# Addition - Easy

## William S. Rogers III

iUniverse, Inc.
Bloomington

# Addition - Easy

iUniverse books may be ordered through booksellers or by contacting:

iUniverse
1663 Liberty Drive
Bloomington, IN 47403
www.iuniverse.com
1-800-Authors (1-800-288-4677)

ISBN: 978-1-4697-3228-2 (sc)
ISBN: 978-1-4697-3229-9 (ebk)

Printed in the United States of America

iUniverse rev. date: 12/29/2011

# CORRELATIONS

Dear Consumer,

**Congratulations**! You have just purchased a one of a kind puzzle that is geared towards education while also having fun. I have worked diligently to create a style of puzzle that is different from the rest and that would stand out easily above all the others. Correlations is a puzzle that is educational and equipped to enhance the minds of others. This style of puzzle originated out of the thought of making math fun. I wanted to create a puzzle that would help people learn or re-learn the basic math concepts and create different levels in which people could try to conquer. Correlations is suitable for all ages of people whether young or old. This puzzle can be formatted for those who want to take it easy and for those who like a little challenge.

Correlations is like an enhanced mathematical word search. I have enjoyed bringing this new style of puzzle to the market, and I hope you enjoy doing this puzzle as much as I have enjoyed creating it. Nothing is too hard to do if you just set your mind to it. Correlations is going to challenge you when it comes to math and searching for the words within the puzzle. Congratulations once again, and I hope you have a blast on your Correlations journey!

**William S. Rogers III**

# How to Solve Correlations

- The puzzles consist of a 7x7 grid
- Solve the math within the box and try to figure out what letters go where
- You do this by knowing where each letter falls in the alphabet (EX: A=1, K=11, P=16, T=20)
- EX: To find the letter B you would look for 1+1. This comes out to equal 2=B
- Once you figure this out you have to find the words within the puzzle
- EX: GREEK – the words are not all straight or diagonal. As long as the G is touching the R box, the R is touching the E box, the E is touching the E box, and the E is touching the K box then the word is found within the puzzle
- The letters within the puzzles are only used once (**NO ONE LETTER OR BOX CAN BE USED TWICE**)
- All the boxes within the puzzle are not to be filled
- (1) (2) (3) (4) – These are used to identify the words on the Answer Sheets

Take this 7 X 7-square example on this page

| | | | | | | |
|---|---|---|---|---|---|---|
| 12+3 | 4+5 | 16+3 | 14+4 | 6+5 | 7+2 | 2+0=B (4) |
| 3+4 | 2+2=D (2) | 10+4=N (2) | 4+1 | 22+3=Y (4) | 1+0=A (4) | 8+6 |
| 9+10 | 1+0=A (2) | 3+3 | 1+2=C (2) | 2+3=E (2) | 14+4=R (4) | 9+2=K (4) |
| 15+5 | 12+2 | 11+6 | 10+5=O (1) | 7+1 | 4+1=E (4) | 16+5 |
| 14+4 | 11+4=O (3) | 4+5=I (1) | 4+1=E (3) | 6+7=M (1) | 5+6 | 17+5 |
| 12+12=X (3) | 1+8 | 1+1=B (3) | 11+8=S (1) | 5+6=K (3) | 13+8=U (3) | 9+2 |
| 5+5 | 6+12 | 1+4 | 5+2 | 12+8=T (1) | 3+4 | 5+5=J (3) |

## WORDS

1. MOIST (13, 15, 9, 19, 20)
2. DANCE  (4, 1, 14, 3, 5)
3. JUKEBOX (10, 21, 11, 5, 2, 15, 24)
4. BAKERY (2, 1, 11, 5, 18, 25)

To start, look for a word that have letters that are not in the other words. The word JUKEBOX; locate the J first by finding 2 numbers that add up to 10. Starting off there are 2 boxes in this puzzle with the sum of 10; in the lower left hand corner and in the lower right hand corner. The one in the right hand corner is the only one that has the letter U connected to it with 13+8. After this there are 3 boxes which contains multiples that equal K. 9+2 to the right, 5+6 up above, and 5+6 to the left. When a situation like this arises in a puzzle, the best thing to do is to plan ahead and look for the other letters in order to figure out which way you should go. So the letter E is connected to 2 K boxes; the one up above and the one to the left. Keep planning ahead and you will discover that the B box is only connected to one of the pathways. Therefore, the K box on the left of the U box is the correct choice. Once that K is found the E is diagonal from that box with 4+1. The B box in which we had to plan ahead for is than diagonal from that box. From the B box the O as well as the X is diagonal from each other. The word JUKEBOX is now found within the puzzle. All the letters have to connect in order for the word to be found within the puzzle. In cases like trying to find the word JUKEBOX, plan ahead and locate other letters within the word you are trying to find. After the word JUKEBOX is found use the Elimination Process (finding a word and not being able to reuse those same boxes over again) if another problem arises like this one.

If one discovers that a word is too hard to find, locate part of the word within the puzzle first, stop, and search for a new word. This often helps because searching for a new word can eliminate some of the boxes that you may have thought were going to be used for the first word you were searching for. There is no guess work that needs to be done when it comes to these puzzles. All you have to do is solve the math, plan ahead, look at the surrounding boxes, and figure out where the words are within the puzzle. Use these tips in order to continue finding the rest of the words within the puzzle.

## Additional Tips

- Try to solve the math within the box to find the words within the puzzle
- Try and look for letters that are not in other words
- In puzzles that have similar letters within words, try and find the letters that are the same (It sometimes help to look for a word backwards, starting with the last letter in the word)
- Remember, you can only use a box once; so try and plan ahead

# EASY

| | | | | | | |
|---|---|---|---|---|---|---|
| 10+10 | 1+2 | 12+11 | 14+3 | 5+5 | 6+12 | 19+1 |
| 4+3 | 5+12 | 12+12 | 1+0 | 5+4 | 10+10 | 11+12 |
| 11+11 | 2+1 | 9+11 | 1+1 | 13+4 | 2+1 | 16+2 |
| 15+11 | 3+2 | 3+3 | 15+3 | 10+5 | 14+4 | 4+1 |
| 13+6 | 9+9 | 14+2 | 1+0 | 11+7 | 4+3 | 12+8 |
| 17+6 | 5+3 | 4+5 | 12+8 | 7+7 | 14+4 | 12+4 |
| 5+5 | 10+10 | 1+1 | 1+0 | 1+2 | 3+2 | 15+1 |

## WORDS

1. FAITH
2. CORRECT
3. BANGER
4. WATERS

## EASY

| | | | | | | |
|---|---|---|---|---|---|---|
| 12+11 | 3+4 | 1+4 | 12+6 | 17+2 | 15+4 | 1+0 |
| 1+0 | 11+8 | 8+7 | 5+2 | 12+2 | 2+1 | 12+6 |
| 2+2 | 15+3 | 12+8 | 8+8 | 5+4 | 2+1 | 5+4 |
| 3+2 | 3+1 | 10+8 | 5+6 | 3+2 | 12+3 | 14+3 |
| 17+2 | 7+2 | 6+6 | 6+3 | 18+5 | 8+4 | 9+8 |
| 13+7 | 1+0 | 10+5 | 8+7 | 6+7 | 10+10 | 11+2 |
| 14+5 | 7+2 | 15+8 | 8+6 | 3+4 | 17+2 | 12+11 |

WORDS

1. ACCEPT
2. MIRRORS
3. WALKING
4. ADDITION

# EASY

| | | | | | | |
|---|---|---|---|---|---|---|
| 2+1 | 10+12 | 2+2 | 14+7 | 6+6 | 11+5 | 16+2 |
| 4+4 | 4+2 | 8+8 | 3+2 | 12+5 | 1+0 | 12+12 |
| 10+10 | 1+0 | 16+7 | 4+5 | 3+2 | 18+2 | 15+5 |
| 19+4 | 12+2 | 4+1 | 10+2 | 7+7 | 3+1 | 4+1 |
| 6+3 | 13+1 | 4+3 | 7+5 | 1+0 | 7+9 | 14+3 |
| 3+4 | 3+2 | 10+9 | 4+1 | 3+2 | 8+5 | 12+1 |
| 5+6 | 5+7 | 10+8 | 10+3 | 12+3 | 15+10 | 1+1 |

WORDS

1. RENEWED
2. MANIPULATE
3. CHANGES
4. YELLED

# EASY

| 12+2 | 16+2 | 11+8 | 15+4 | 5+7 | 8+1 | 10+10 |
|------|------|------|------|------|------|-------|
| 11+2 | 3+2 | 10+9 | 12+1 | 3+4 | 1+1 | 16+1 |
| 5+2 | 3+2 | 2+2 | 14+5 | 5+6 | 10+10 | 4+3 |
| 12+2 | 10+8 | 21+4 | 15+3 | 19+3 | 15+3 | 15+6 |
| 7+2 | 7+8 | 12+8 | 14+7 | 3+2 | 13+13 | 4+5 |
| 13+13 | 11+3 | 11+2 | 6+3 | 3+2 | 21+2 | 5+5 |
| 17+3 | 3+3 | 12+12 | 10+4 | 1+0 | 5+1 | 7+4 |

WORDS

1. MURDERS
2. WAITRESS
3. GREEN
4. ZONING

**EASY**

| | | | | | | |
|---|---|---|---|---|---|---|
| 10+6 | 3+2 | 4+5 | 12+12 | 6+4 | 7+8 | 10+10 |
| 1+0 | 4+4 | 12+6 | 18+1 | 15+3 | 17+4 | 14+4 |
| 2+1 | 14+2 | 11+12 | 13+2 | 12+2 | 23+2 | 15+1 |
| 14+7 | 1+0 | 3+2 | 14+5 | 5+4 | 6+4 | 9+8 |
| 7+8 | 1+0 | 11+7 | 2+1 | 9+6 | 6+3 | 8+6 |
| 4+1 | 7+7 | 1+0 | 2+0 | 10+4 | 15+3 | 12+3 |
| 16+5 | 7+2 | 11+11 | 6+3 | 2+2 | 17+3 | 8+4 |

WORDS

1. PAPERS
2. BREACH
3. INDIANA
4. UNICORN

# EASY

| 18+3 | 12+7 | 9+3 | 10+10 | 14+3 | 11+11 | 12+4 |
|------|------|-----|-------|------|-------|------|
| 17+4 | 6+4 | 10+6 | 7+2 | 19+2 | 17+2 | 15+6 |
| 5+5 | 11+4 | 3+2 | 17+3 | 11+5 | 10+5 | 4+4 |
| 12+6 | 5+6 | 20+5 | 11+8 | 1+1 | 2+1 | 14+5 |
| 12+8 | 10+9 | 10+3 | 3+2 | 9+2 | 1+0 | 1+1 |
| 14+3 | 15+4 | 1+0 | 1+0 | 6+6 | 16+4 | 14+7 |
| 11+4 | 13+2 | 2+0 | 8+4 | 4+1 | 10+10 | 10+9 |

WORDS

1. BASKETBALL
2. HOCKEY
3. TEAMS
4. SPORTS

# EASY

| | | | | | | |
|---|---|---|---|---|---|---|
| 5+4 | 12+3 | 11+11 | 22+3 | 16+3 | 6+4 | 10+10 |
| 9+8 | 14+1 | 18+2 | 4+1 | 16+2 | 19+0 | 3+4 |
| 12+9 | 4+5 | 3+1 | 3+2 | 12+6 | 21+2 | 20+4 |
| 12+2 | 1+2 | 15+5 | 3+2 | 1+0 | 11+9 | 12+4 |
| 1+0 | 10+2 | 10+4 | 15+3 | 7+2 | 14+7 | 12+7 |
| 7+8 | 14+5 | 7+2 | 6+3 | 6+7 | 3+2 | 14+3 |
| 11+2 | 15+4 | 6+4 | 4+2 | 7+4 | 12+12 | 10+9 |

## WORDS

1. INSANITY
2. TIMES
3. SQUARED
4. FILTERS

## EASY

| 10+8 | 12+4 | 7+2 | 6+2 | 10+10 | 17+3 | 15+4 |
|------|------|------|------|-------|------|------|
| 3+2 | 2+2 | 9+6 | 5+6 | 2+1 | 5+5 | 15+4 |
| 7+7 | 11+4 | 11+1 | 10+3 | 1+0 | 2+1 | 10+8 |
| 13+2 | 7+5 | 5+5 | 7+2 | 5+3 | 3+2 | 4+1 |
| 6+1 | 10+10 | 14+6 | 6+3 | 12+2 | 2+2 | 8+4 |
| 10+10 | 17+8 | 17+4 | 11+4 | 4+5 | 1+1 | 9+2 |
| 15+4 | 1+1 | 11+4 | 4+5 | 16+7 | 6+7 | 17+3 |

## WORDS

1. CHILDREN
2. BLEACH
3. OUTLOOK
4. WONDERS

## EASY

| | | | | | | |
|---|---|---|---|---|---|---|
| 5+4 | 11+12 | 3+4 | 11+2 | 12+4 | 10+10 | 5+6 |
| 7+5 | 6+5 | 12+12 | 4+5 | 4+1 | 21+2 | 10+9 |
| 3+3 | 1+1 | 14+11 | 15+3 | 17+2 | 2+1 | 4+2 |
| 8+7 | 4+6 | 2+3 | 11+8 | 8+2 | 16+2 | 9+8 |
| 10+4 | 12+12 | 12+6 | 3+2 | 1+0 | 1+0 | 5+4 |
| 7+3 | 5+4 | 4+1 | 3+1 | 11+1 | 1+1 | 16+4 |
| 20+4 | 15+4 | 10+3 | 6+7 | 1+1 | 7+6 | 8+1 |

WORDS

1. FOXES
2. ADMIRE
3. SCRABBLE
4. MESSY

## EASY

| | | | | | | |
|---|---|---|---|---|---|---|
| 4+1 | 2+1 | 6+4 | 11+11 | 14+5 | 4+3 | 10+6 |
| 2+3 | 10+6 | 18+3 | 10+10 | 12+4 | 11+7 | 3+4 |
| 10+2 | 8+7 | 2+2 | 1+1 | 11+4 | 4+1 | 5+6 |
| 14+4 | 2+2 | 6+6 | 7+8 | 5+4 | 11+3 | 9+9 |
| 8+1 | 2+3 | 14+1 | 3+2 | 11+11 | 8+6 | 12+6 |
| 16+5 | 9+7 | 15+2 | 15+3 | 8+8 | 4+1 | 5+6 |
| 11+13 | 5+6 | 17+4 | 18+4 | 9+1 | 10+10 | 12+7 |

## WORDS

1. CUDDLE
2. PROPER
3. ENVELOPE
4. SENIORS

# EASY

| | | | | | | |
|---|---|---|---|---|---|---|
| 4+5 | 16+4 | 5+6 | 16+3 | 12+12 | 10+9 | 5+6 |
| 11+3 | 4+1 | 10+1 | 10+5 | 6+2 | 1+0 | 17+8 |
| 9+4 | 2+1 | 11+5 | 4+1 | 15+6 | 6+7 | 8+1 |
| 10+5 | 5+4 | 3+2 | 4+1 | 2+1 | 4+2 | 1+1 |
| 17+2 | 5+6 | 10+4 | 2+1 | 10+8 | 1+0 | 5+1 |
| 10+4 | 7+7 | 10+5 | 7+4 | 10+2 | 4+4 | 14+6 |
| 13+5 | 17+3 | 8+1 | 4+5 | 6+1 | 14+6 | 12+5 |

WORDS

1. SAUCE
2. KNICKS
3. FALCONS
4. THREE

**EASY**

| | | | | | | |
|---|---|---|---|---|---|---|
| 5+4 | 11+3 | 11+7 | 5+6 | 4+1 | 10+4 | 17+4 |
| 19+3 | 4+1 | 21+3 | 11+1 | 4+3 | 23+2 | 5+3 |
| 12+2 | 12+8 | 15+5 | 1+0 | 15+5 | 11+4 | 2+2 |
| 10+3 | 4+4 | 2+1 | 12+8 | 11+4 | 4+5 | 17+2 |
| 16+4 | 7+2 | 5+4 | 1+0 | 3+2 | 8+7 | 4+4 |
| 2+1 | 4+4 | 10+4 | 15+7 | 5+2 | 16+3 | 7+3 |
| 18+3 | 15+3 | 7+3 | 7+4 | 3+1 | 7+2 | 14+4 |

WORDS

1. CHICAGO
2. SEATTLE
3. RETHINK
4. SHOOT

# EASY

| 11+5 | 6+4 | 7+6 | 19+4 | 10+5 | 6+7 | 17+2 |
|------|------|------|------|------|------|------|
| 18+2 | 9+7 | 5+4 | 12+2 | 10+10 | 11+4 | 12+12 |
| 13+12 | 7+5 | 3+2 | 13+1 | 11+13 | 15+4 | 5+3 |
| 19+2 | 21+3 | 5+8 | 2+1 | 10+1 | 8+8 | 10+10 |
| 1+1 | 4+3 | 5+6 | 5+5 | 1+0 | 5+6 | 9+4 |
| 4+3 | 1+0 | 2+2 | 1+0 | 3+2 | 13+2 | 12+5 |
| 16+5 | 12+2 | 7+2 | 7+7 | 14+4 | 12+11 | 10+6 |

WORDS

1. ADJACENT
2. WEAK
3. LINKS
4. MORNING

**EASY**

| 10+4 | 5+1 | 16+4 | 17+1 | 3+2 | 7+5 | 14+6 |
|------|------|------|------|------|------|------|
| 6+5 | 8+8 | 9+6 | 10+3 | 14+3 | 10+10 | 12+12 |
| 21+3 | 10+9 | 1+0 | 5+3 | 3+2 | 4+1 | 3+2 |
| 7+1 | 3+2 | 2+2 | 19+3 | 10+2 | 10+10 | 8+3 |
| 13+5 | 13+2 | 16+4 | 3+1 | 15+4 | 9+6 | 8+7 |
| 11+11 | 5+4 | 11+1 | 4+3 | 12+8 | 17+2 | 10+10 |
| 16+8 | 4+1 | 16+4 | 22+3 | 3+5 | 6+1 | 1+1 |

WORDS

1. PADDLE
2. TIRESOME
3. STYLE
4. KETTLE

**EASY**

| 5+4 | 16+7 | 8+3 | 9+3 | 4+3 | 11+12 | 14+2 |
|-----|------|-----|-----|-----|-------|------|
| 2+1 | 11+11 | 12+10 | 1+0 | 7+3 | 6+1 | 17+3 |
| 19+2 | 10+8 | 15+5 | 3+1 | 5+3 | 12+4 | 10+9 |
| 17+3 | 1+0 | 3+2 | 18+4 | 4+1 | 9+4 | 3+2 |
| 12+1 | 2+2 | 2+2 | 6+6 | 12+2 | 15+7 | 13+5 |
| 6+1 | 6+3 | 7+7 | 3+2 | 13+7 | 7+2 | 15+3 |
| 13+9 | 17+7 | 11+1 | 4+5 | 11+12 | 16+3 | 16+1 |

WORDS

1. CRADLE
2. WIVES
3. GATED
4. LINEN

# EASY

| | | | | | | |
|---|---|---|---|---|---|---|
| 15+4 | 6+2 | 10+10 | 6+4 | 18+1 | 17+1 | 16+3 |
| 1+1 | 19+3 | 15+3 | 5+2 | 5+4 | 6+7 | 3+2 |
| 5+6 | 10+9 | 10+2 | 12+8 | 6+3 | 5+2 | 1+0 |
| 3+2 | 16+5 | 2+2 | 15+3 | 12+6 | 11+4 | 18+2 |
| 14+4 | 4+4 | 3+1 | 8+4 | 15+3 | 4+1 | 13+4 |
| 21+3 | 8+7 | 23+1 | 15+4 | 4+5 | 6+5 | 10+10 |
| 18+3 | 19+5 | 10+10 | 17+2 | 11+5 | 6+1 | 12+5 |

WORDS

1. GIRLS
2. ULTIMATE
3. STORES
4. KROGERS

# EASY

| 7+5 | 6+4 | 12+4 | 12+12 | 6+3 | 10+5 | 19+4 |
|------|-------|-------|-------|------|------|------|
| 4+5 | 17+3 | 11+4 | 10+9 | 13+4 | 14+5 | 17+2 |
| 14+4 | 11+5 | 6+6 | 5+6 | 12+2 | 12+8 | 4+3 |
| 1+0 | 7+2 | 12+4 | 6+7 | 5+4 | 14+1 | 8+6 |
| 17+3 | 10+12 | 3+2 | 10+3 | 18+4 | 6+3 | 5+4 |
| 8+5 | 9+0 | 12+3 | 11+7 | 15+4 | 14+4 | 1+0 |
| 10+10 | 5+3 | 2+1 | 10+4 | 6+1 | 12+8 | 17+2 |

WORDS

1. VERSIONS
2. TRAIL
3. COMMIT
4. STRINGS

# EASY

| | | | | | | |
|---|---|---|---|---|---|---|
| 6+1 | 4+3 | 16+2 | 9+3 | 17+3 | 19+2 | 2+1 |
| 12+4 | 5+5 | 3+2 | 4+1 | 6+6 | 10+5 | 11+4 |
| 11+13 | 10+3 | 4+3 | 11+8 | 12+7 | 5+3 | 10+9 |
| 7+8 | 4+3 | 11+4 | 3+2 | 12+8 | 9+3 | 5+2 |
| 2+2 | 2+3 | 12+2 | 15+5 | 14+4 | 10+0 | 6+4 |
| 14+4 | 21+4 | 3+2 | 1+0 | 14+5 | 4+1 | 17+2 |
| 18+2 | 13+2 | 4+1 | 16+3 | 13+5 | 16+4 | 7+4 |

WORDS

1. STRANGER
2. REMOTE
3. JERSEY
4. COLLEGES

# EASY

| 4+5 | 10+4 | 1+0 | 6+4 | 17+1 | 17+2 | 9+9 |
|-----|------|-----|-----|------|------|-----|
| 8+6 | 8+8 | 12+12 | 3+1 | 13+5 | 3+2 | 15+3 |
| 4+5 | 8+7 | 5+4 | 10+6 | 15+7 | 14+3 | 4+1 |
| 18+2 | 11+7 | 17+3 | 3+2 | 8+5 | 7+6 | 21+3 |
| 23+3 | 11+4 | 5+5 | 15+5 | 11+2 | 14+1 | 6+1 |
| 11+11 | 3+5 | 7+5 | 7+2 | 1+0 | 1+2 | 7+4 |
| 17+3 | 12+7 | 11+12 | 4+2 | 11+4 | 4+4 | 19+4 |

WORDS

1. COMPTON
2. FLORIDA
3. WHATEVER
4. SWIMMERS

## EASY

| 5+1 | 12+4 | 10+8 | 16+3 | 12+12 | 4+5 | 7+3 |
|-----|------|------|------|-------|-----|-----|
| 10+2 | 4+1 | 1+0 | 1+0 | 10+10 | 5+3 | 16+2 |
| 15+7 | 3+2 | 3+1 | 1+1 | 3+2 | 11+5 | 6+1 |
| 6+3 | 8+6 | 15+6 | 12+4 | 4+4 | 13+5 | 14+5 |
| 2+2 | 2+1 | 7+7 | 14+7 | 10+8 | 11+4 | 4+1 |
| 10+10 | 9+7 | 15+4 | 4+0 | 10+10 | 9+4 | 11+11 |
| 3+3 | 11+4 | 12+5 | 14+1 | 11+9 | 8+1 | 8+7 |

WORDS

1. SCUBA
2. TUNNEL
3. DIVERS
4. OVERHEAD

# EASY

| | | | | | | |
|---|---|---|---|---|---|---|
| 6+4 | 12+12 | 4+5 | 10+10 | 1+1 | 17+4 | 10+5 |
| 5+2 | 5+6 | 17+2 | 6+7 | 2+1 | 4+3 | 7+7 |
| 11+5 | 11+3 | 12+5 | 2+2 | 12+2 | 4+1 | 7+6 |
| 9+8 | 7+2 | 8+8 | 8+6 | 3+3 | 5+4 | 10+7 |
| 14+6 | 15+4 | 14+7 | 3+2 | 10+8 | 6+6 | 5+2 |
| 10+9 | 14+1 | 21+2 | 1+1 | 10+2 | 3+2 | 9+7 |
| 6+3 | 7+2 | 11+5 | 15+5 | 4+4 | 5+2 | 13+4 |

WORDS

1. SPELLING
2. POUNDS
3. PERFECT
4. TWISTING

**EASY**

| | | | | | | |
|---|---|---|---|---|---|---|
| 12+3 | 4+2 | 10+4 | 6+4 | 17+2 | 11+8 | 1+1 |
| 10+10 | 5+3 | 8+5 | 3+2 | 12+2 | 10+10 | 3+2 |
| 14+3 | 17+4 | 7+1 | 1+0 | 10+4 | 4+3 | 11+3 |
| 2+1 | 2+2 | 5+3 | 5+4 | 12+2 | 3+2 | 18+4 |
| 17+3 | 10+5 | 8+8 | 2+1 | 14+10 | 5+2 | 10+9 |
| 15+3 | 11+5 | 2+2 | 3+0 | 15+3 | 4+1 | 6+3 |
| 1+1 | 3+4 | 6+3 | 4+4 | 13+6 | 19+2 | 6+1 |

WORDS

1. DOCUMENTS
2. EXCHANGE
3. SHIPPING
4. CRUISE

# EASY

| | | | | | | |
|---|---|---|---|---|---|---|
| 5+6 | 14+6 | 7+3 | 17+3 | 14+3 | 7+1 | 10+10 |
| 6+2 | 12+3 | 1+0 | 3+2 | 12+12 | 11+4 | 10+3 |
| 4+1 | 1+1 | 8+4 | 15+5 | 14+4 | 14+4 | 11+7 |
| 16+4 | 9+6 | 2+1 | 14+7 | 8+7 | 6+5 | 23+2 |
| 8+7 | 4+1 | 12+8 | 10+4 | 3+2 | 1+0 | 16+3 |
| 21+3 | 12+6 | 3+2 | 12+8 | 16+3 | 20+5 | 9+6 |
| 16+3 | 16+2 | 6+3 | 3+1 | 14+10 | 1+2 | 22+2 |

WORDS

1. TURKEY
2. DIRECTORY
3. COASTERS
4. TABLE

# EASY

| | | | | | | |
|---|---|---|---|---|---|---|
| 1+2 | 5+4 | 8+8 | 15+5 | 4+3 | 11+3 | 12+12 |
| 10+10 | 1+0 | 5+3 | 7+7 | 1+0 | 10+10 | 7+3 |
| 9+8 | 8+4 | 5+4 | 4+1 | 12+2 | 6+3 | 9+7 |
| 8+7 | 10+6 | 12+7 | 11+4 | 21+2 | 10+4 | 20+3 |
| 16+5 | 4+1 | 14+4 | 7+2 | 4+4 | 19+3 | 16+3 |
| 10+2 | 10+8 | 11+11 | 13+5 | 15+6 | 2+1 | 24+1 |
| 1+1 | 3+2 | 14+2 | 12+4 | 1+0 | 6+7 | 4+4 |

WORDS

1. PRESENT
2. CHIRPING
3. CAPTAINS
4. MARVEL

# EASY

| | | | | | | |
|---|---|---|---|---|---|---|
| 3+2 | 2+1 | 14+5 | 10+8 | 4+3 | 4+4 | 12+4 |
| 6+1 | 15+7 | 15+3 | 6+2 | 3+2 | 17+7 | 9+7 |
| 10+10 | 3+2 | 14+4 | 12+13 | 6+3 | 8+7 | 8+1 |
| 13+4 | 5+4 | 1+0 | 21+4 | 1+1 | 2+1 | 2+2 |
| 3+3 | 13+7 | 7+5 | 4+3 | 10+8 | 9+6 | 19+6 |
| 10+6 | 11+7 | 15+10 | 11+5 | 14+7 | 4+1 | 9+5 |
| 15+3 | 6+2 | 12+8 | 8+6 | 1+1 | 12+8 | 1+0 |

## WORDS

1. PLAYERS
2. COUNTRY
3. EVERYBODY
4. GREAT

# EASY

| | | | | | | |
|---|---|---|---|---|---|---|
| 14+5 | 6+3 | 12+2 | 5+2 | 2+2 | 5+6 | 10+10 |
| 7+2 | 17+3 | 15+7 | 19+2 | 9+7 | 3+2 | 13+5 |
| 8+7 | 1+0 | 12+1 | 3+2 | 15+3 | 11+8 | 3+2 |
| 5+3 | 5+5 | 15+5 | 13+10 | 21+3 | 6+5 | 2+1 |
| 14+10 | 1+0 | 4+1 | 17+5 | 10+3 | 4+1 | 12+8 |
| 1+1 | 20+2 | 15+3 | 11+4 | 5+4 | 11+11 | 10+5 |
| 15+11 | 16+3 | 5+4 | 16+4 | 17+2 | 8+8 | 6+1 |

WORDS

1. MOTIVATE
2. DESKTOP
3. HAVING
4. RECEIVE

# EASY

| | | | | | | |
|---|---|---|---|---|---|---|
| 6+2 | 2+1 | 10+4 | 16+3 | 12+3 | 13+1 | 15+3 |
| 11+12 | 7+4 | 17+4 | 5+4 | 15+10 | 9+2 | 6+3 |
| 21+4 | 14+5 | 10+10 | 15+5 | 1+1 | 4+1 | 4+4 |
| 17+2 | 12+1 | 12+8 | 19+2 | 7+7 | 9+8 | 10+2 |
| 13+6 | 14+7 | 14+4 | 2+1 | 17+3 | 12+12 | 14+6 |
| 15+7 | 8+7 | 12+3 | 5+4 | 3+2 | 14+7 | 21+3 |
| 23+3 | 4+2 | 4+1 | 7+6 | 5+5 | 12+12 | 3+2 |

WORDS

1. TIMEOUT
2. KENTUCKY
3. EXECUTION
4. FORMS

**EASY**

| | | | | | | |
|------|------|-------|------|------|-------|--------|
| 12+4 | 15+3 | 11+6 | 14+6 | 5+4 | 18+2 | 10+10 |
| 14+4 | 4+1 | 15+7 | 17+2 | 1+0 | 19+2 | 1+0 |
| 13+5 | 2+2 | 3+2 | 10+5 | 14+3 | 15+8 | 5+5 |
| 13+2 | 1+1 | 8+6 | 4+4 | 16+2 | 13+2 | 11+11 |
| 13+12 | 14+3 | 10+8 | 3+2 | 17+2 | 11+8 | 2+1 |
| 19+4 | 15+3 | 16+3 | 14+7 | 15+5 | 6+3 | 11+8 |
| 15+3 | 11+4 | 18+4 | 6+4 | 7+1 | 10+13 | 9+6 |

WORDS

1. TURNOVER
2. SCORES
3. WISHES
4. AWAIT

# EASY

| | | | | | | |
|---|---|---|---|---|---|---|
| 7+6 | 15+3 | 14+7 | 2+0 | 7+5 | 10+10 | 4+3 |
| 5+6 | 8+8 | 3+2 | 5+3 | 5+4 | 12+2 | 5+5 |
| 13+12 | 13+11 | 14+6 | 21+4 | 1+0 | 2+1 | 12+8 |
| 13+4 | 7+7 | 5+6 | 6+6 | 5+2 | 6+3 | 7+1 |
| 4+1 | 18+2 | 4+3 | 5+4 | 10+4 | 2+1 | 10+10 |
| 8+5 | 11+11 | 8+8 | 6+3 | 1+0 | 9+8 | 12+11 |
| 12+12 | 7+4 | 4+1 | 11+8 | 17+3 | 11+2 | 12+5 |

WORDS

1. GIGANTIC
2. SEVENTH
3. MAINLY
4. REPUBLIC

# EASY

| | | | | | | |
|---|---|---|---|---|---|---|
| 11+5 | 6+1 | 17+4 | 14+2 | 5+2 | 12+2 | 14+6 |
| 9+8 | 9+5 | 12+3 | 9+9 | 5+5 | 16+3 | 5+4 |
| 11+3 | 12+12 | 17+4 | 10+3 | 4+1 | 10+10 | 8+4 |
| 1+1 | 16+2 | 1+0 | 14+4 | 1+1 | 10+2 | 12+7 |
| 19+3 | 7+5 | 2+2 | 14+4 | 3+2 | 12+3 | 1+0 |
| 3+3 | 3+2 | 4+1 | 10+5 | 12+12 | 12+2 | 1+1 |
| 20+4 | 4+6 | 7+2 | 6+7 | 5+4 | 12+4 | 17+2 |

WORDS

1. DOMINOS
2. NUMBER
3. FLARES
4. BALLING

# EASY

| | | | | | | |
|---|---|---|---|---|---|---|
| 9+2 | 12+3 | 15+4 | 17+2 | 16+3 | 11+12 | 12+13 |
| 5+4 | 2+0 | 4+1 | 1+1 | 12+4 | 2+1 | 10+10 |
| 7+6 | 13+4 | 18+3 | 12+2 | 14+4 | 10+5 | 19+3 |
| 7+1 | 15+4 | 14+6 | 5+4 | 21+1 | 9+8 | 17+2 |
| 15+4 | 12+4 | 9+7 | 10+10 | 3+2 | 8+6 | 11+4 |
| 4+1 | 1+0 | 7+2 | 4+1 | 8+7 | 12+6 | 10+10 |
| 13+4 | 18+2 | 6+2 | 5+6 | 5+2 | 1+0 | 11+3 |

## WORDS

1. COVERAGE
2. BUTTONS
3. HAPPINESS
4. KITES

# EASY

| | | | | | | |
|---|---|---|---|---|---|---|
| 1+0 | 10+4 | 15+7 | 8+7 | 19+3 | 11+12 | 12+14 |
| 6+2 | 15+4 | 16+3 | 4+1 | 11+12 | 1+0 | 11+3 |
| 5+4 | 6+1 | 13+7 | 14+7 | 12+8 | 7+5 | 11+4 |
| 10+6 | 17+3 | 6+6 | 1+0 | 7+7 | 18+4 | 8+6 |
| 5+5 | 8+7 | 11+1 | 5+4 | 11+5 | 11+8 | 4+3 |
| 16+3 | 16+1 | 9+3 | 20+2 | 16+3 | 8+6 | 3+2 |
| 7+2 | 6+1 | 7+3 | 1+0 | 6+3 | 12+7 | 18+1 |

WORDS

1. LIVING
2. WALNUTS
3. ISOLATE
4. GLASSES

# EASY

| 17+2 | 11+3 | 10+10 | 10+9 | 5+6 | 8+2 | 9+1 |
|------|------|-------|------|-----|-----|-----|
| 12+13 | 4+1 | 12+6 | 6+7 | 4+4 | 8+1 | 11+4 |
| 9+9 | 8+5 | 15+4 | 8+7 | 3+2 | 10+6 | 17+3 |
| 10+9 | 3+2 | 16+4 | 4+1 | 2+2 | 13+5 | 4+4 |
| 1+1 | 12+7 | 21+4 | 3+2 | 12+4 | 8+8 | 1+0 |
| 23+2 | 4+3 | 11+9 | 16+2 | 14+4 | 10+3 | 9+6 |
| 12+4 | 5+3 | 6+8 | 15+5 | 3+2 | 1+1 | 10+8 |

WORDS

1. PRETTY
2. SHEETS
3. BOARDER
4. ROSES

## EASY

| | | | | | | |
|---|---|---|---|---|---|---|
| 14+11 | 5+8 | 7+2 | 4+3 | 17+2 | 8+9 | 10+11 |
| 15+4 | 13+9 | 4+1 | 9+3 | 17+1 | 19+2 | 11+5 |
| 2+3 | 6+6 | 10+2 | 1+0 | 13+2 | 8+3 | 1+0 |
| 10+4 | 1+0 | 13+3 | 5+4 | 11+2 | 5+1 | 12+2 |
| 13+3 | 4+1 | 5+4 | 16+3 | 16+1 | 7+2 | 17+2 |
| 9+8 | 14+4 | 6+7 | 10+10 | 1+0 | 12+3 | 12+12 |
| 10+10 | 14+5 | 13+11 | 15+5 | 14+2 | 5+3 | 6+8 |

WORDS

1. TRIPLE
2. OATMEAL
3. FORGIVEN
4. ANIMALS

# EASY

| | | | | | | |
|---|---|---|---|---|---|---|
| 6+5 | 3+3 | 11+4 | 18+1 | 3+2 | 5+1 | 16+3 |
| 10+10 | 11+3 | 10+5 | 12+11 | 15+3 | 14+5 | 2+1 |
| 13+5 | 3+2 | 13+8 | 6+3 | 12+7 | 5+3 | 15+3 |
| 7+7 | 11+1 | 14+6 | 10+8 | 12+8 | 9+6 | 7+4 |
| 9+5 | 11+4 | 10+10 | 8+8 | 17+4 | 10+14 | 15+2 |
| 11+4 | 2+2 | 5+4 | 1+0 | 1+1 | 1+0 | 15+10 |
| 14+10 | 5+3 | 12+2 | 10+3 | 1+7 | 7+3 | 8+2 |

## WORDS

1. FOURTH
2. MITTEN
3. ABANDON
4. CROSSES

## EASY

| | | | | | | |
|---|---|---|---|---|---|---|
| 12+4 | 5+2 | 12+8 | 10+10 | 10+1 | 10+9 | 11+4 |
| 17+2 | 1+0 | 11+8 | 4+1 | 3+1 | 8+3 | 3+2 |
| 14+2 | 8+6 | 5+6 | 6+7 | 11+3 | 12+7 | 4+4 |
| 12+3 | 2+1 | 5+4 | 5+5 | 1+0 | 12+12 | 16+3 |
| 6+4 | 8+7 | 10+3 | 12+10 | 15+10 | 6+7 | 7+2 |
| 12+12 | 1+0 | 17+2 | 14+11 | 6+7 | 16+4 | 18+2 |
| 7+5 | 6+6 | 7+2 | 1+0 | 19+4 | 3+2 | 1+1 |

## WORDS

1. VASES
2. SOCKS
3. LAMINATE
4. EMAIL

# EASY

| | | | | | | |
|---|---|---|---|---|---|---|
| 6+1 | 7+7 | 4+5 | 16+2 | 18+3 | 10+10 | 6+3 |
| 4+3 | 5+4 | 6+7 | 14+3 | 2+2 | 11+12 | 14+3 |
| 11+3 | 4+1 | 3+2 | 13+3 | 14+4 | 7+2 | 11+2 |
| 10+8 | 12+1 | 15+3 | 3+2 | 6+6 | 2+2 | 15+5 |
| 16+3 | 11+4 | 1+0 | 14+9 | 8+4 | 3+2 | 10+10 |
| 11+8 | 1+1 | 4+2 | 14+7 | 4+3 | 1+0 | 17+3 |
| 19+5 | 5+1 | 3+3 | 4+1 | 2+1 | 14+10 | 11+5 |

WORDS

1. FOREIGN
2. CUFFS
3. DREAMERS
4. MILEAGE

**EASY**

| | | | | | | |
|---|---|---|---|---|---|---|
| 11+12 | 4+5 | 7+4 | 2+1 | 4+4 | 10+2 | 10+10 |
| 17+3 | 9+4 | 1+0 | 14+2 | 3+2 | 8+6 | 13+10 |
| 3+2 | 12+3 | 3+1 | 15+7 | 9+6 | 10+3 | 9+9 |
| 8+6 | 10+9 | 11+7 | 12+8 | 1+0 | 18+8 | 10+8 |
| 16+5 | 16+3 | 13+6 | 12+2 | 12+6 | 4+1 | 11+12 |
| 11+11 | 1+1 | 3+2 | 13+2 | 5+2 | 15+5 | 18+3 |
| 10+5 | 7+4 | 9+5 | 1+1 | 8+6 | 17+3 | 11+3 |

WORDS

1. BOSTON
2. MESSENGER
3. TRAVEL
4. ROACH

**EASY**

| | | | | | | |
|---|---|---|---|---|---|---|
| 6+8 | 10+10 | 2+2 | 14+2 | 17+3 | 2+1 | 6+6 |
| 5+5 | 17+3 | 8+8 | 12+11 | 10+15 | 11+7 | 14+10 |
| 16+4 | 16+1 | 14+4 | 3+4 | 13+2 | 18+4 | 4+1 |
| 15+3 | 7+7 | 2+3 | 5+5 | 10+8 | 3+2 | 2+1 |
| 15+11 | 5+3 | 8+7 | 6+7 | 4+2 | 5+4 | 5+2 |
| 14+7 | 18+4 | 14+6 | 1+0 | 19+5 | 17+3 | 10+10 |
| 14+8 | 7+1 | 19+3 | 11+12 | 11+4 | 10+4 | 13+11 |

WORDS

1. FATHER
2. VERMONT
3. NOTICE
4. CROWD

**EASY**

| 11+5 | 6+3 | 15+6 | 11+7 | 15+5 | 10+10 | 14+2 |
|------|------|------|------|------|-------|------|
| 14+10 | 8+8 | 10+5 | 14+2 | 5+6 | 9+9 | 15+7 |
| 6+2 | 6+6 | 4+3 | 8+8 | 8+6 | 10+10 | 3+3 |
| 7+2 | 7+1 | 7+7 | 10+3 | 1+0 | 11+7 | 17+2 |
| 15+9 | 12+2 | 10+4 | 6+3 | 1+0 | 1+1 | 15+8 |
| 2+2 | 14+8 | 3+2 | 1+1 | 7+5 | 11+4 | 15+6 |
| 5+3 | 12+11 | 5+4 | 10+2 | 14+7 | 11+9 | 6+6 |

WORDS

1. TRAMPOLINE
2. TUBING
3. WILLOWS
4. BANKRUPT

# EASY

| | | | | | | |
|---|---|---|---|---|---|---|
| 22+2 | 15+3 | 1+1 | 11+12 | 17+2 | 4+1 | 19+2 |
| 10+10 | 3+2 | 1+5 | 13+5 | 5+2 | 17+5 | 16+2 |
| 7+2 | 2+1 | 12+10 | 10+10 | 3+2 | 7+7 | 4+1 |
| 8+7 | 8+8 | 3+2 | 8+6 | 3+11 | 16+3 | 5+4 |
| 5+4 | 13+1 | 3+1 | 15+4 | 10+10 | 1+1 | 7+5 |
| 18+5 | 16+3 | 10+4 | 11+1 | 5+5 | 4+1 | 11+4 |
| 10+10 | 11+1 | 3+2 | 5+4 | 1+0 | 16+4 | 1+1 |

WORDS

1. OBSERVE
2. INNOCENT
3. TALES
4. BELIEVE

## EASY

| 5+4 | 17+2 | 19+3 | 10+11 | 15+3 | 14+10 | 4+3 |
|------|------|------|-------|------|-------|------|
| 11+4 | 16+4 | 1+1 | 15+3 | 1+0 | 18+2 | 16+2 |
| 4+4 | 1+0 | 14+2 | 8+8 | 5+3 | 14+6 | 4+1 |
| 2+2 | 13+9 | 18+3 | 12+8 | 6+3 | 11+5 | 21+3 |
| 24+1 | 7+5 | 3+0 | 1+0 | 10+3 | 12+3 | 10+10 |
| 11+12 | 15+10 | 4+1 | 2+1 | 7+7 | 1+0 | 14+11 |
| 7+2 | 5+3 | 8+8 | 10+5 | 9+1 | 12+10 | 1+2 |

WORDS

1. OCCUPATION
2. BADLY
3. HEATH
4. CAMPER

# EASY

| | | | | | | |
|---|---|---|---|---|---|---|
| 5+4 | 15+6 | 10+10 | 14+5 | 11+12 | 16+4 | 17+2 |
| 17+5 | 2+2 | 14+4 | 19+3 | 5+2 | 15+11 | 11+4 |
| 4+4 | 3+2 | 1+0 | 3+1 | 10+4 | 11+12 | 17+2 |
| 5+2 | 12+12 | 17+8 | 6+3 | 2+2 | 1+0 | 4+1 |
| 6+3 | 12+2 | 5+2 | 1+0 | 8+6 | 6+3 | 14+7 |
| 6+2 | 6+3 | 4+3 | 11+7 | 20+5 | 11+10 | 5+2 |
| 1+1 | 15+6 | 4+4 | 10+10 | 10+6 | 11+1 | 12+5 |

## WORDS

1. PRAYERS
2. ANYTHING
3. HUGGING
4. DADDIES

**EASY**

| | | | | | | |
|---|---|---|---|---|---|---|
| 17+3 | 19+3 | 3+2 | 17+2 | 12+2 | 9+9 | 10+11 |
| 13+5 | 4+3 | 16+3 | 4+3 | 17+2 | 5+4 | 12+12 |
| 5+5 | 4+1 | 1+0 | 16+2 | 1+1 | 8+4 | 12+6 |
| 4+4 | 8+4 | 10+5 | 6+7 | 6+6 | 18+3 | 13+2 |
| 5+4 | 2+1 | 10+3 | 1+0 | 12+4 | 1+0 | 14+10 |
| 10+10 | 15+6 | 17+4 | 9+3 | 3+1 | 4+4 | 3+0 |
| 6+7 | 17+3 | 14+4 | 12+3 | 2+1 | 13+11 | 8+1 |

WORDS

1. DAMAGES
2. RUMORS
3. CALLING
4. COUCHES

**EASY**

| 11+12 | 5+6 | 10+10 | 6+4 | 18+4 | 19+3 | 12+5 |
|-------|------|-------|------|-------|------|-------|
| 15+4 | 4+5 | 5+2 | 11+3 | 12+14 | 2+1 | 16+4 |
| 17+3 | 4+1 | 10+8 | 3+1 | 1+0 | 19+4 | 10+10 |
| 12+13 | 11+4 | 5+2 | 7+7 | 10+4 | 5+3 | 1+1 |
| 4+5 | 10+9 | 15+6 | 1+0 | 2+2 | 14+6 | 8+4 |
| 14+10 | 17+2 | 4+1 | 7+5 | 6+7 | 5+4 | 1+1 |
| 6+7 | 16+2 | 10+10 | 4+4 | 5+2 | 7+2 | 11+11 |

WORDS

1. CANDLES
2. LIGHTS
3. GROUND
4. IMAGES

# EASY

| | | | | | | |
|------|------|------|------|------|-------|------|
| 6+1 | 16+4 | 18+2 | 7+1 | 4+3 | 3+2 | 17+8 |
| 17+2 | 11+4 | 13+3 | 7+2 | 14+4 | 12+12 | 5+2 |
| 20+3 | 14+4 | 8+4 | 2+2 | 1+0 | 3+3 | 12+2 |
| 5+5 | 12+4 | 3+2 | 5+3 | 4+1 | 17+4 | 10+6 |
| 16+8 | 8+1 | 5+2 | 10+3 | 11+5 | 10+2 | 8+7 |
| 11+3 | 1+1 | 12+3 | 5+4 | 4+1 | 12+2 | 21+4 |
| 4+5 | 15+8 | 16+1 | 18+4 | 5+3 | 18+5 | 5+2 |

WORDS

1. LEADERS
2. HIGHLIGHT
3. WOMEN
4. YOUNGER

# EASY

| | | | | | | |
|---|---|---|---|---|---|---|
| 11+12 | 4+5 | 16+5 | 3+1 | 12+2 | 14+7 | 11+10 |
| 7+2 | 5+2 | 3+2 | 4+1 | 8+8 | 10+4 | 7+3 |
| 8+6 | 16+3 | 16+2 | 14+2 | 16+3 | 5+4 | 10+10 |
| 12+13 | 5+4 | 5+6 | 9+7 | 2+2 | 6+4 | 15+8 |
| 13+4 | 12+10 | 10+5 | 7+2 | 1+0 | 15+3 | 21+2 |
| 9+7 | 15+3 | 1+0 | 9+6 | 11+1 | 10+5 | 16+10 |
| 6+5 | 1+1 | 11+4 | 16+3 | 18+3 | 11+3 | 1+1 |

WORDS

1. LOOKING
2. BRAIDS
3. WRAPPED
4. WINNERS

**EASY**

| | | | | | | |
|---|---|---|---|---|---|---|
| 10+10 | 6+4 | 9+7 | 4+4 | 10+5 | 17+3 | 11+11 |
| 14+11 | 12+13 | 1+0 | 9+6 | 2+1 | 3+1 | 16+2 |
| 2+1 | 1+0 | 17+2 | 15+4 | 16+2 | 3+2 | 16+2 |
| 4+1 | 11+5 | 6+6 | 4+1 | 10+10 | 14+7 | 1+0 |
| 6+12 | 15+4 | 13+3 | 17+3 | 19+5 | 11+5 | 8+7 |
| 21+3 | 4+3 | 5+5 | 3+2 | 10+6 | 1+1 | 10+10 |
| 1+1 | 2+1 | 7+5 | 5+4 | 14+4 | 12+12 | 15+3 |

WORDS

1. REPLACE
2. PURCHASE
3. CLIPBOARD
4. POSTER

# EASY

| | | | | | | |
|---|---|---|---|---|---|---|
| 7+7 | 15+3 | 17+2 | 10+10 | 11+12 | 15+3 | 10+10 |
| 14+5 | 11+2 | 5+4 | 10+8 | 15+10 | 3+2 | 11+11 |
| 9+1 | 5+2 | 14+4 | 12+3 | 8+4 | 14+7 | 6+6 |
| 8+2 | 1+1 | 12+3 | 6+3 | 7+7 | 4+3 | 7+3 |
| 17+2 | 12+12 | 3+2 | 1+1 | 19+5 | 12+2 | 15+3 |
| 18+3 | 3+2 | 14+6 | 6+6 | 4+1 | 2+1 | 1+0 |
| 10+9 | 10+12 | 15+9 | 13+4 | 17+2 | 8+8 | 10+11 |

WORDS

1. BOXES
2. CELEBRITY
3. SPANGLE
4. JUNIOR

**EASY**

| | | | | | | |
|---|---|---|---|---|---|---|
| 11+12 | 5+6 | 1+0 | 8+5 | 18+4 | 10+10 | 10+2 |
| 7+3 | 14+7 | 15+11 | 15+3 | 16+4 | 1+0 | 18+2 |
| 10+14 | 12+6 | 4+5 | 10+8 | 2+1 | 6+6 | 17+3 |
| 12+4 | 17+2 | 1+0 | 8+7 | 7+2 | 11+4 | 17+2 |
| 9+2 | 3+2 | 2+1 | 12+8 | 21+2 | 13+6 | 5+2 |
| 1+1 | 5+4 | 17+4 | 6+7 | 14+1 | 8+6 | 11+12 |
| 3+3 | 2+2 | 10+3 | 16+2 | 7+2 | 8+5 | 13+9 |

WORDS

1. PRACTICAL
2. MOMMIES
3. DURING
4. ARROWS

# EASY

| | | | | | | |
|---|---|---|---|---|---|---|
| 15+6 | 23+1 | 10+10 | 3+3 | 16+3 | 18+4 | 19+2 |
| 2+2 | 14+12 | 4+2 | 15+6 | 15+3 | 5+5 | 10+12 |
| 4+1 | 15+5 | 12+8 | 17+4 | 7+8 | 3+2 | 8+3 |
| 9+9 | 5+4 | 1+0 | 15+9 | 5+2 | 16+3 | 10+1 |
| 1+1 | 14+2 | 2+0 | 6+3 | 17+3 | 4+4 | 8+2 |
| 5+5 | 16+7 | 11+2 | 1+1 | 10+5 | 5+4 | 10+10 |
| 14+3 | 11+7 | 1+0 | 1+1 | 1+1 | 6+6 | 15+11 |

WORDS

1. MIXTURES
2. LOBBIED
3. RABBI
4. TAUGHT

# EASY

| | | | | | | |
|---|---|---|---|---|---|---|
| 14+3 | 1+0 | 19+3 | 11+6 | 18+3 | 4+4 | 10+10 |
| 4+4 | 1+0 | 16+2 | 4+3 | 6+6 | 12+2 | 4+1 |
| 14+6 | 2+1 | 12+4 | 11+13 | 3+2 | 7+4 | 16+2 |
| 4+3 | 11+4 | 1+1 | 14+4 | 15+6 | 2+1 | 3+2 |
| 19+3 | 16+4 | 5+6 | 5+2 | 15+3 | 4+4 | 6+3 |
| 11+12 | 9+5 | 1+0 | 15+3 | 13+7 | 10+2 | 4+2 |
| 10+6 | 17+5 | 8+7 | 3+1 | 18+6 | 12+12 | 2+1 |

## WORDS

1. CHARGER
2. DAKOTA
3. NORTHERN
4. CLICK

# EASY

| 14+5 | 18+3 | 11+12 | 5+4 | 7+7 | 10+10 | 13+10 |
|------|------|-------|-----|-----|-------|-------|
| 2+0 | 4+3 | 17+2 | 12+4 | 5+2 | 4+5 | 7+1 |
| 16+5 | 3+2 | 14+3 | 3+2 | 10+4 | 4+2 | 1+1 |
| 11+11 | 2+2 | 5+2 | 5+4 | 9+3 | 17+2 | 12+14 |
| 14+3 | 15+4 | 3+1 | 8+6 | 2+2 | 8+1 | 11+2 |
| 13+6 | 18+7 | 19+4 | 7+2 | 12+2 | 10+10 | 19+4 |
| 4+4 | 5+2 | 10+8 | 1+0 | 7+4 | 11+4 | 25+1 |

WORDS

1. BEDDING
2. KINGS
3. MILES
4. GRANDS

## EASY

| 12+12 | 4+3 | 6+6 | 11+8 | 10+9 | 10+11 | 19+3 |
|-------|-----|-----|------|------|-------|------|
| 4+3 | 16+3 | 12+3 | 20+3 | 2+1 | 18+5 | 16+3 |
| 1+1 | 3+1 | 11+11 | 13+2 | 4+4 | 12+13 | 8+6 |
| 11+13 | 9+5 | 4+1 | 5+3 | 12+3 | 1+0 | 5+5 |
| 3+3 | 14+4 | 7+2 | 10+4 | 10+5 | 10+3 | 10+10 |
| 14+3 | 15+7 | 21+2 | 6+6 | 2+1 | 5+4 | 18+9 |
| 19+4 | 10+11 | 14+3 | 1+1 | 5+3 | 5+2 | 13+1 |

WORDS

1. FRENCH
2. NAMING
3. SCHOOL
4. WINDOWS

## EASY

| | | | | | | |
|---|---|---|---|---|---|---|
| 7+3 | 12+13 | 5+5 | 14+5 | 4+1 | 17+6 | 19+4 |
| 12+12 | 5+6 | 10+9 | 5+3 | 10+10 | 2+2 | 11+12 |
| 12+13 | 3+2 | 4+6 | 2+1 | 4+4 | 17+9 | 10+5 |
| 14+4 | 14+1 | 4+3 | 10+4 | 4+1 | 5+2 | 1+1 |
| 11+11 | 8+8 | 8+2 | 12+2 | 6+3 | 15+6 | 21+4 |
| 20+3 | 3+5 | 13+11 | 6+3 | 13+3 | 10+6 | 1+0 |
| 16+7 | 8+1 | 2+1 | 4+1 | 7+7 | 10+10 | 10+2 |

WORDS

1. PINCHED
2. EXPRESS
3. LAUGH
4. ICING

# EASY

| | | | | | | |
|---|---|---|---|---|---|---|
| 15+4 | 5+2 | 13+1 | 1+1 | 16+3 | 10+4 | 4+3 |
| 5+6 | 11+1 | 21+3 | 5+4 | 5+1 | 5+4 | 20+3 |
| 3+3 | 18+4 | 4+1 | 12+8 | 1+1 | 7+5 | 19+3 |
| 2+2 | 23+2 | 17+2 | 4+1 | 12+10 | 3+2 | 21+3 |
| 12+12 | 13+5 | 11+8 | 10+10 | 16+9 | 1+0 | 12+11 |
| 11+4 | 13+6 | 14+7 | 8+7 | 2+2 | 12+3 | 1+1 |
| 9+7 | 8+9 | 3+2 | 6+3 | 9+11 | 12+5 | 6+3 |

WORDS

1. YOURSELF
2. BODIES
3. LEAVES
4. GIFTING

# EASY

| 11+11 | 1+0 | 4+5 | 10+10 | 4+3 | 17+5 | 8+8 |
|-------|-----|-----|-------|-----|------|-----|
| 17+4 | 9+3 | 11+11 | 12+11 | 13+5 | 11+3 | 21+3 |
| 8+6 | 20+3 | 14+6 | 3+2 | 8+7 | 10+3 | 15+3 |
| 13+4 | 14+6 | 10+2 | 15+4 | 6+3 | 4+1 | 4+4 |
| 15+5 | 5+4 | 4+1 | 2+1 | 4+1 | 6+6 | 5+5 |
| 12+12 | 15+7 | 3+2 | 7+7 | 1+0 | 18+1 | 13+12 |
| 11+13 | 17+2 | 5+4 | 12+8 | 15+6 | 5+3 | 16+7 |

WORDS

1. UNCLE
2. AUNTIES
3. RELATIVE
4. NOISES

**EASY**

| | | | | | | |
|---|---|---|---|---|---|---|
| 5+6 | 7+11 | 12+13 | 9+9 | 10+10 | 12+1 | 11+1 |
| 1+1 | 12+4 | 16+3 | 12+4 | 10+9 | 5+6 | 12+12 |
| 11+13 | 21+3 | 17+2 | 6+3 | 8+6 | 10+1 | 20+3 |
| 10+10 | 6+6 | 2+1 | 21+2 | 2+1 | 5+6 | 7+3 |
| 1+0 | 9+9 | 9+6 | 5+6 | 1+0 | 4+1 | 8+8 |
| 13+12 | 15+7 | 10+8 | 14+11 | 7+5 | 16+2 | 10+4 |
| 4+4 | 4+6 | 13+2 | 5+2 | 6+2 | 12+11 | 16+4 |

WORDS

1. PICKLE
2. OVALS
3. TRACK
4. GROWN

# EASY

| | | | | | | |
|---|---|---|---|---|---|---|
| 7+9 | 9+11 | 12+11 | 14+5 | 17+4 | 18+4 | 12+12 |
| 5+5 | 4+3 | 1+1 | 10+10 | 11+11 | 13+1 | 16+9 |
| 10+3 | 15+0 | 12+1 | 2+2 | 1+0 | 5+5 | 16+3 |
| 15+5 | 13+5 | 6+3 | 10+10 | 7+4 | 3+2 | 4+1 |
| 10+12 | 12+2 | 13+1 | 12+2 | 12+3 | 11+7 | 12+2 |
| 20+4 | 7+2 | 10+5 | 5+2 | 4+4 | 9+6 | 17+3 |
| 12+12 | 11+4 | 14+5 | 12+8 | 13+13 | 5+3 | 7+7 |

WORDS

1. KNOTS
2. JOINING
3. TREAT
4. ZONES

# EASY

| | | | | | | |
|---|---|---|---|---|---|---|
| 12+11 | 10+4 | 8+8 | 17+2 | 11+13 | 5+3 | 1+1 |
| 12+3 | 10+10 | 14+3 | 8+1 | 21+4 | 12+1 | 1+0 |
| 15+11 | 6+3 | 15+6 | 7+7 | 10+10 | 6+6 | 7+5 |
| 12+12 | 15+5 | 11+7 | 6+7 | 11+13 | 6+3 | 10+2 |
| 11+11 | 1+0 | 18+3 | 1+1 | 11+2 | 3+2 | 19+4 |
| 4+4 | 13+7 | 2+1 | 1+0 | 15+3 | 15+2 | 12+6 |
| 17+4 | 1+0 | 17+5 | 19+5 | 5+1 | 8+7 | 7+7 |

WORDS

1. FAMILY
2. UMBRELLA
3. TURNIPS
4. VACATION

# EASY

| 5+3 | 16+3 | 8+6 | 10+8 | 4+1 | 11+11 | 12+7 |
|---|---|---|---|---|---|---|
| 10+10 | 9+9 | 2+1 | 3+2 | 16+2 | 8+5 | 7+7 |
| 15+3 | 6+6 | 7+2 | 14+12 | 4+1 | 16+1 | 10+10 |
| 3+2 | 17+2 | 5+4 | 10+2 | 1+0 | 12+13 | 15+2 |
| 14+10 | 13+11 | 18+6 | 1+0 | 10+4 | 15+3 | 11+7 |
| 5+5 | 6+4 | 1+0 | 12+3 | 3+2 | 5+3 | 1+1 |
| 10+13 | 14+3 | 5+2 | 20+3 | 23+1 | 2+2 | 22+0 |

WORDS

1. BRAZIL
2. WAXES
3. DEALER
4. SCREEN

**EASY**

| | | | | | | |
|---|---|---|---|---|---|---|
| 7+3 | 2+1 | 6+3 | 7+7 | 17+2 | 19+3 | 7+3 |
| 4+1 | 10+12 | 14+5 | 10+10 | 17+2 | 16+5 | 11+13 |
| 13+4 | 14+4 | 5+6 | 12+7 | 5+4 | 9+11 | 12+5 |
| 5+5 | 4+3 | 3+2 | 12+2 | 11+11 | 12+12 | 5+8 |
| 9+5 | 1+1 | 11+4 | 6+1 | 10+10 | 10+2 | 19+3 |
| 21+3 | 24+2 | 16+3 | 11+3 | 3+2 | 4+4 | 15+5 |
| 18+4 | 17+8 | 5+6 | 8+8 | 14+7 | 15+3 | 2+2 |

WORDS

1. GOSPEL
2. SINGERS
3. DRUNK
4. JUSTICE

# EASY

| 14+4 | 5+4 | 3+2 | 11+11 | 10+5 | 10+10 | 11+12 |
|------|-----|-----|-------|------|-------|-------|
| 13+12 | 11+7 | 14+6 | 2+2 | 15+10 | 11+3 | 5+2 |
| 5+5 | 17+2 | 4+1 | 12+2 | 7+2 | 10+4 | 6+6 |
| 8+7 | 9+3 | 4+4 | 16+2 | 4+5 | 12+3 | 6+4 |
| 13+13 | 12+4 | 1+0 | 12+8 | 12+7 | 12+12 | 6+3 |
| 10+5 | 7+1 | 4+1 | 10+2 | 10+5 | 6+3 | 1+1 |
| 11+8 | 17+3 | 16+3 | 18+3 | 1+1 | 19+4 | 1+0 |

WORDS

1. BOTHERED
2. JOINTS
3. SHARING
4. AISLES

**EASY**

| | | | | | | |
|---|---|---|---|---|---|---|
| 10+10 | 9+5 | 8+3 | 4+5 | 18+1 | 12+12 | 13+11 |
| 11+4 | 11+11 | 21+3 | 14+4 | 4+1 | 20+2 | 14+10 |
| 5+3 | 12+3 | 2+2 | 10+10 | 3+2 | 15+3 | 1+1 |
| 11+11 | 8+7 | 1+0 | 7+5 | 10+10 | 12+5 | 12+12 |
| 10+4 | 3+2 | 12+8 | 3+2 | 13+13 | 12+8 | 4+3 |
| 5+7 | 1+0 | 17+6 | 19+1 | 17+2 | 1+0 | 10+5 |
| 2+1 | 7+7 | 16+3 | 19+3 | 8+4 | 3+2 | 6+7 |

WORDS

1. NOODLES
2. SWEATER
3. MATTERS
4. CATTLE

# EASY

| | | | | | | |
|---|---|---|---|---|---|---|
| 6+5 | 16+2 | 6+6 | 17+2 | 4+1 | 10+10 | 12+3 |
| 1+1 | 3+1 | 1+0 | 12+2 | 3+1 | 8+5 | 12+12 |
| 16+3 | 4+3 | 17+1 | 5+5 | 8+6 | 12+6 | 17+2 |
| 11+11 | 10+10 | 4+1 | 2+1 | 5+3 | 14+1 | 4+1 |
| 9+6 | 1+1 | 15+3 | 11+7 | 7+7 | 2+1 | 10+15 |
| 14+3 | 6+7 | 1+0 | 3+0 | 4+1 | 2+2 | 21+3 |
| 20+4 | 5+5 | 3+2 | 11+2 | 15+10 | 14+3 | 17+7 |

WORDS

1. MARCH
2. DECEMBER
3. SECONDS
4. MENARDS

# EASY

| 5+4 | 10+4 | 9+6 | 5+5 | 16+3 | 18+4 | 19+3 |
|-----|------|-----|-----|------|------|------|
| 11+11 | 5+4 | 4+1 | 8+6 | 10+10 | 12+11 | 14+11 |
| 14+3 | 10+2 | 12+8 | 15+3 | 16+4 | 2+1 | 18+7 |
| 7+5 | 4+4 | 17+4 | 14+5 | 1+0 | 6+6 | 17+6 |
| 15+6 | 12+3 | 3+0 | 17+3 | 4+1 | 19+2 | 13+5 |
| 13+10 | 2+1 | 21+2 | 14+4 | 14+7 | 13+5 | 1+1 |
| 11+11 | 16+3 | 1+0 | 12+4 | 10+10 | 11+6 | 12+14 |

WORDS

1. QUESTION
2. ACCURACY
3. TRULY
4. SWOLLEN

# EASY

| | | | | | | |
|---|---|---|---|---|---|---|
| 5+2 | 17+4 | 10+10 | 3+2 | 11+12 | 15+3 | 17+3 |
| 1+1 | 12+2 | 8+6 | 15+4 | 10+1 | 18+3 | 10+3 |
| 10+10 | 5+4 | 1+0 | 2+1 | 10+10 | 4+4 | 12+6 |
| 6+7 | 4+1 | 9+2 | 2+2 | 7+2 | 7+7 | 10+4 |
| 13+12 | 16+2 | 5+4 | 1+0 | 1+0 | 5+3 | 11+11 |
| 15+10 | 7+7 | 2+0 | 4+4 | 4+1 | 12+5 | 2+1 |
| 6+12 | 4+3 | 18+1 | 12+9 | 17+2 | 6+2 | 10+9 |

WORDS

1. CHICKEN
2. BREAST
3. SHAKING
4. HEADINGS

## EASY

| | | | | | | |
|---|---|---|---|---|---|---|
| 5+11 | 12+12 | 5+6 | 6+3 | 1+1 | 11+12 | 2+1 |
| 10+2 | 1+0 | 13+4 | 16+3 | 18+3 | 9+4 | 19+2 |
| 19+4 | 4+4 | 15+3 | 1+0 | 12+12 | 16+2 | 13+2 |
| 11+11 | 16+6 | 12+8 | 14+7 | 1+1 | 8+4 | 5+5 |
| 10+4 | 10+10 | 14+6 | 15+5 | 17+2 | 12+5 | 15+8 |
| 5+15 | 6+6 | 14+5 | 1+0 | 14+8 | 4+1 | 15+7 |
| 10+12 | 2+3 | 15+10 | 3+2 | 8+6 | 1+0 | 10+4 |

WORDS

1. BATTLE
2. NATURAL
3. WEAVES
4. CURLS

# EASY

| | | | | | | |
|---|---|---|---|---|---|---|
| 4+3 | 16+2 | 12+12 | 4+5 | 13+6 | 5+7 | 13+5 |
| 16+2 | 3+2 | 11+12 | 7+7 | 3+2 | 18+1 | 10+10 |
| 10+10 | 4+1 | 10+4 | 9+3 | 4+5 | 9+5 | 6+11 |
| 10+4 | 3+2 | 2+1 | 20+2 | 11+11 | 1+0 | 4+1 |
| 14+10 | 4+1 | 5+4 | 7+2 | 10+8 | 7+5 | 1+1 |
| 7+6 | 14+6 | 2+1 | 6+6 | 10+2 | 17+3 | 12+14 |
| 21+3 | 4+4 | 16+2 | 1+0 | 12+12 | 21+4 | 15+10 |

WORDS

1. TRAINS
2. CENTER
3. ARTICLES
4. GREENVILLE

# EASY

| | | | | | | |
|---|---|---|---|---|---|---|
| 12+12 | 13+11 | 6+3 | 12+2 | 21+2 | 17+1 | 5+5 |
| 16+7 | 18+3 | 4+3 | 6+5 | 17+2 | 1+1 | 3+2 |
| 9+4 | 10+10 | 4+1 | 11+7 | 8+7 | 2+2 | 8+1 |
| 13+2 | 5+3 | 2+2 | 17+3 | 9+6 | 7+7 | 10+2 |
| 11+13 | 12+12 | 3+2 | 2+1 | 14+4 | 15+5 | 1+0 |
| 16+2 | 1+0 | 10+10 | 1+0 | 1+1 | 11+11 | 12+5 |
| 5+5 | 3+1 | 17+4 | 17+2 | 6+6 | 19+2 | 10+10 |

WORDS

1. COOKING
2. STARTERS
3. VANDERBILT
4. HEARD

# EASY

| | | | | | | |
|---|---|---|---|---|---|---|
| 4+3 | 15+5 | 4+1 | 11+12 | 14+5 | 10+10 | 5+3 |
| 1+1 | 13+2 | 12+12 | 12+8 | 8+6 | 5+6 | 7+2 |
| 14+5 | 3+2 | 1+0 | 7+2 | 8+7 | 19+1 | 20+2 |
| 21+2 | 11+7 | 21+4 | 8+8 | 16+2 | 5+2 | 12+12 |
| 16+7 | 18+4 | 3+2 | 7+7 | 9+3 | 11+5 | 18+1 |
| 12+12 | 18+2 | 18+4 | 4+1 | 1+1 | 13+11 | 11+12 |
| 4+5 | 5+6 | 8+4 | 10+2 | 4+5 | 10+9 | 10+5 |

WORDS

1. WEAPON
2. BELT
3. SPRITE
4. SILVER

**EASY**

| | | | | | | |
|---|---|---|---|---|---|---|
| 6+3 | 12+12 | 14+7 | 1+1 | 10+6 | 5+5 | 10+10 |
| 15+4 | 11+12 | 1+5 | 1+0 | 7+3 | 5+3 | 2+1 |
| 7+7 | 9+8 | 18+1 | 10+11 | 12+1 | 1+0 | 12+11 |
| 13+5 | 10+9 | 16+4 | 12+7 | 11+5 | 5+4 | 13+13 |
| 10+6 | 14+4 | 12+6 | 3+2 | 16+2 | 13+6 | 21+1 |
| 2+2 | 3+2 | 1+0 | 14+7 | 10+10 | 4+1 | 13+13 |
| 12+11 | 1+1 | 13+5 | 12+4 | 1+0 | 10+4 | 16+3 |

WORDS

1. PAMPERS
2. APARTS
3. VENTURED
4. CHAIRS

# EASY

| 12+11 | 1+1 | 15+4 | 10+10 | 7+4 | 6+6 | 4+12 |
|-------|-----|------|-------|-----|-----|------|
| 15+5 | 12+12 | 5+3 | 10+9 | 6+6 | 10+10 | 3+4 |
| 7+1 | 4+4 | 15+3 | 1+1 | 11+11 | 12+14 | 16+4 |
| 11+11 | 10+9 | 8+7 | 15+8 | 4+1 | 6+6 | 13+11 |
| 3+2 | 7+2 | 1+1 | 14+4 | 6+6 | 10+12 | 2+0 |
| 8+4 | 14+4 | 12+11 | 11+7 | 3+2 | 5+6 | 6+3 |
| 7+2 | 3+1 | 11+3 | 13+8 | 1+1 | 4+4 | 12+12 |

## WORDS

1. ERRORS
2. BLEW
3. IRISH
4. BUNDLE

**EASY**

| 13+13 | 1+0 | 4+3 | 1+1 | 11+12 | 13+11 | 14+10 |
|-------|-----|-----|-----|-------|-------|-------|
| 7+4 | 10+10 | 17+1 | 3+2 | 4+4 | 15+6 | 17+3 |
| 19+3 | 2+1 | 15+4 | 4+1 | 13+2 | 5+2 | 16+2 |
| 2+2 | 1+0 | 12+12 | 2+2 | 7+7 | 3+2 | 13+5 |
| 5+5 | 10+10 | 8+8 | 7+2 | 1+0 | 7+3 | 19+4 |
| 18+7 | 7+2 | 1+0 | 15+3 | 12+3 | 4+4 | 10+4 |
| 10+10 | 10+2 | 9+7 | 15+4 | 11+7 | 1+0 | 3+2 |

WORDS

1. PACKAGES
2. HOSPITAL
3. READER
4. EARRING

# EASY

| | | | | | | |
|---|---|---|---|---|---|---|
| 1+1 | 4+1 | 4+3 | 8+6 | 17+2 | 12+12 | 10+9 |
| 13+13 | 11+3 | 13+2 | 3+0 | 4+4 | 4+1 | 13+6 |
| 9+3 | 7+2 | 5+4 | 10+10 | 2+1 | 3+2 | 12+12 |
| 7+12 | 5+6 | 8+1 | 12+8 | 1+0 | 11+8 | 14+5 |
| 15+10 | 17+3 | 11+7 | 11+5 | 10+10 | 14+4 | 17+4 |
| 16+3 | 19+5 | 10+5 | 1+0 | 12+12 | 1+1 | 13+12 |
| 11+4 | 1+1 | 6+4 | 2+2 | 7+4 | 5+5 | 12+9 |

## WORDS

1. OPTIONS
2. BRACES
3. DARKING
4. STITCHES

## EASY

| | | | | | | |
|---|---|---|---|---|---|---|
| 3+3 | 16+5 | 11+11 | 12+12 | 10+10 | 4+5 | 6+2 |
| 8+1 | 14+3 | 8+3 | 1+0 | 16+5 | 3+2 | 16+3 |
| 14+4 | 10+9 | 6+6 | 15+10 | 10+9 | 14+4 | 4+5 |
| 12+4 | 14+2 | 5+3 | 3+2 | 12+8 | 18+7 | 14+7 |
| 8+7 | 8+8 | 6+7 | 15+4 | 12+14 | 3+0 | 15+3 |
| 17+3 | 9+5 | 1+0 | 4+1 | 17+3 | 19+5 | 3+0 |
| 6+6 | 17+3 | 10+10 | 14+11 | 13+13 | 10+5 | 1+1 |

WORDS

1. FISHES
2. TEMPLATE
3. NASTY
4. OCCURS

**EASY**

| 14+3 | 5+5 | 13+6 | 12+12 | 10+4 | 10+10 | 15+5 |
|------|-----|------|-------|------|-------|------|
| 17+3 | 9+3 | 3+2 | 4+1 | 7+2 | 5+3 | 19+5 |
| 15+7 | 10+9 | 1+0 | 11+3 | 3+2 | 10+9 | 17+4 |
| 16+3 | 1+1 | 4+3 | 2+1 | 6+1 | 15+4 | 3+3 |
| 5+4 | 3+2 | 12+12 | 12+3 | 16+2 | 14+5 | 13+5 |
| 7+6 | 8+6 | 11+1 | 7+7 | 9+5 | 16+5 | 9+5 |
| 11+12 | 14+3 | 12+2 | 4+1 | 13+7 | 4+4 | 10+10 |

WORDS

1. THINGS
2. LOCALS
3. TENNESSEE
4. NURSES

**EASY**

| | | | | | | |
|---|---|---|---|---|---|---|
| 12+10 | 1+1 | 4+5 | 6+1 | 16+3 | 19+3 | 12+12 |
| 11+4 | 4+1 | 15+5 | 21+3 | 12+2 | 13+13 | 18+1 |
| 3+3 | 12+6 | 1+0 | 6+3 | 12+12 | 4+1 | 5+6 |
| 7+3 | 15+4 | 15+5 | 1+1 | 6+2 | 17+2 | 11+11 |
| 13+11 | 14+10 | 1+0 | 3+2 | 4+1 | 16+3 | 10+10 |
| 8+9 | 10+5 | 6+6 | 21+1 | 6+2 | 9+9 | 1+0 |
| 12+9 | 6+4 | 22+1 | 6+6 | 12+12 | 7+5 | 2+2 |

WORDS

1. FEARS
2. HEATING
3. WOLVES
4. LASHES

# EASY

| 10+2 | 11+12 | 14+3 | 9+7 | 5+5 | 10+10 | 11+11 |
|------|-------|------|-----|-----|-------|-------|
| 12+12 | 4+1 | 13+3 | 14+4 | 11+11 | 5+5 | 19+3 |
| 13+3 | 1+0 | 11+4 | 3+3 | 4+1 | 6+1 | 1+1 |
| 5+6 | 8+5 | 7+4 | 5+3 | 6+6 | 2+1 | 15+4 |
| 11+13 | 12+6 | 7+2 | 12+13 | 4+5 | 6+7 | 11+1 |
| 5+4 | 4+2 | 4+1 | 8+6 | 4+3 | 1+0 | 4+1 |
| 7+6 | 8+5 | 14+11 | 8+4 | 10+2 | 11+12 | 1+1 |

WORDS

1. LEAKING
2. SMALLER
3. VEHICLE
4. PROM

**EASY**

| | | | | | | |
|---|---|---|---|---|---|---|
| 16+5 | 1+1 | 7+7 | 10+10 | 7+2 | 1+1 | 12+12 |
| 14+1 | 13+3 | 11+5 | 5+3 | 6+6 | 20+6 | 1+1 |
| 12+8 | 1+0 | 10+10 | 9+4 | 15+4 | 12+6 | 13+13 |
| 18+2 | 2+1 | 11+2 | 7+8 | 3+2 | 5+2 | 14+7 |
| 13+2 | 8+7 | 7+2 | 10+3 | 5+4 | 7+7 | 2+1 |
| 14+5 | 7+5 | 4+1 | 4+2 | 7+2 | 1+0 | 10+10 |
| 11+12 | 13+11 | 10+10 | 4+4 | 12+12 | 5+6 | 8+2 |

WORDS

1. SOMETHING
2. PACIFIER
3. JACUZZI
4. BOTTOM

# EASY

| | | | | | | |
|---|---|---|---|---|---|---|
| 5+12 | 11+12 | 4+5 | 13+6 | 10+10 | 5+3 | 1+1 |
| 5+4 | 17+2 | 4+2 | 17+2 | 2+1 | 19+5 | 16+3 |
| 17+4 | 13+12 | 4+1 | 5+0 | 4+1 | 12+7 | 11+12 |
| 11+11 | 2+1 | 10+10 | 14+4 | 10+4 | 6+5 | 14+11 |
| 20+3 | 3+2 | 10+9 | 15+1 | 3+2 | 12+2 | 5+4 |
| 16+8 | 15+3 | 8+1 | 8+8 | 1+0 | 13+1 | 12+12 |
| 11+8 | 13+13 | 17+2 | 4+2 | 21+4 | 11+1 | 11+11 |

## WORDS

1. CEREAL
2. SISTERS
3. SKINNY
4. SCENE

**EASY**

| | | | | | | |
|---|---|---|---|---|---|---|
| 15+3 | 3+2 | 13+11 | 12+12 | 5+3 | 14+5 | 4+3 |
| 11+10 | 16+3 | 11+8 | 5+2 | 10+1 | 8+6 | 10+10 |
| 13+11 | 10+10 | 3+1 | 5+5 | 10+4 | 5+1 | 7+2 |
| 2+1 | 8+8 | 12+2 | 5+4 | 9+6 | 10+8 | 6+1 |
| 6+3 | 12+12 | 10+1 | 3+2 | 5+4 | 11+12 | 12+2 |
| 9+7 | 11+11 | 16+3 | 4+5 | 16+4 | 6+3 | 18+3 |
| 10+5 | 19+7 | 12+12 | 1+0 | 15+10 | 11+7 | 5+5 |

WORDS

1. FRIENDS
2. ASKING
3. RINGING
4. PICTURES

# EASY

| | | | | | | |
|---|---|---|---|---|---|---|
| 11+12 | 16+4 | 7+4 | 7+7 | 11+2 | 10+10 | 19+4 |
| 4+3 | 12+3 | 14+5 | 11+5 | 12+12 | 7+2 | 13+5 |
| 13+13 | 8+6 | 5+3 | 2+1 | 11+11 | 4+4 | 1+1 |
| 6+4 | 6+2 | 8+1 | 7+3 | 1+0 | 14+2 | 17+6 |
| 16+8 | 19+3 | 10+10 | 21+2 | 8+5 | 11+4 | 16+3 |
| 3+3 | 1+0 | 15+3 | 4+1 | 11+4 | 10+4 | 18+1 |
| 14+5 | 4+2 | 10+8 | 8+7 | 7+7 | 12+8 | 9+2 |

## WORDS

1. CAMERA
2. WHIMPS
3. KNOWING
4. FRONTS

**EASY**

| | | | | | | |
|---|---|---|---|---|---|---|
| 15+5 | 1+1 | 12+4 | 14+3 | 6+4 | 10+10 | 11+12 |
| 11+11 | 4+4 | 13+1 | 12+12 | 7+7 | 4+1 | 9+8 |
| 8+9 | 15+3 | 10+9 | 1+1 | 5+5 | 2+3 | 12+12 |
| 15+4 | 5+4 | 12+2 | 12+7 | 2+2 | 11+6 | 7+4 |
| 1+1 | 4+4 | 10+2 | 7+2 | 9+5 | 4+1 | 12+6 |
| 14+7 | 13+9 | 7+5 | 13+7 | 15+8 | 21+2 | 18+2 |
| 20+4 | 9+1 | 6+2 | 11+9 | 13+7 | 12+12 | 14+5 |

WORDS

1. TWINS
2. WEEDS
3. THRILL
4. TENTH

# EASY

| | | | | | | |
|---|---|---|---|---|---|---|
| 15+4 | 11+8 | 1+1 | 14+5 | 7+6 | 16+2 | 19+3 |
| 11+12 | 1+4 | 1+0 | 10+4 | 2+2 | 1+0 | 16+3 |
| 17+5 | 14+5 | 3+2 | 11+1 | 8+8 | 19+4 | 10+1 |
| 10+10 | 4+3 | 16+4 | 8+4 | 10+2 | 3+2 | 5+4 |
| 12+12 | 15+3 | 8+7 | 7+5 | 1+0 | 2+1 | 16+3 |
| 13+4 | 12+8 | 5+1 | 11+7 | 3+2 | 14+6 | 6+2 |
| 18+1 | 5+5 | 21+3 | 12+6 | 7+7 | 13+5 | 9+0 |

WORDS

1. TALLEST
2. STROLLER
3. RAKES
4. SANDWICH

## EASY

| | | | | | | |
|---|---|---|---|---|---|---|
| 15+6 | 10+9 | 12+12 | 19+3 | 10+10 | 6+1 | 11+3 |
| 5+4 | 6+6 | 6+3 | 12+14 | 11+5 | 9+0 | 11+11 |
| 8+8 | 4+2 | 10+4 | 2+0 | 10+2 | 14+4 | 13+10 |
| 13+4 | 5+8 | 10+2 | 2+1 | 7+2 | 19+3 | 18+3 |
| 21+2 | 1+0 | 5+4 | 12+12 | 9+2 | 4+3 | 1+1 |
| 3+1 | 12+6 | 15+4 | 1+0 | 12+2 | 6+6 | 5+2 |
| 2+2 | 12+4 | 12+8 | 6+3 | 7+7 | 8+1 | 5+3 |

WORDS

1. FLIRTING
2. PRICK
3. DASANI
4. SIBLING

# EASY

| 16+4 | 11+11 | 13+2 | 12+13 | 1+1 | 6+4 | 6+6 |
|------|-------|------|-------|-----|-----|-----|
| 12+13 | 5+4 | 16+3 | 11+3 | 11+8 | 15+4 | 17+2 |
| 10+10 | 15+10 | 11+14 | 4+1 | 16+3 | 3+2 | 3+1 |
| 10+5 | 9+7 | 10+2 | 12+12 | 6+7 | 12+6 | 17+2 |
| 11+3 | 2+0 | 1+0 | 1+1 | 3+2 | 17+5 | 18+3 |
| 19+3 | 14+9 | 9+9 | 3+0 | 12+12 | 4+4 | 10+10 |
| 1+1 | 5+3 | 11+4 | 2+1 | 4+1 | 14+4 | 5+5 |

WORDS

1. BLESSES
2. COWBOY
3. HERDS
4. RECAP

**EASY**

| 10+10 | 5+3 | 1+1 | 11+8 | 9+6 | 14+6 | 11+11 |
|---|---|---|---|---|---|---|
| 13+12 | 12+12 | 19+2 | 16+2 | 18+1 | 13+13 | 1+1 |
| 6+4 | 6+6 | 14+4 | 8+8 | 12+5 | 8+7 | 17+3 |
| 19+4 | 14+7 | 1+0 | 14+1 | 4+4 | 2+1 | 3+1 |
| 1+0 | 2+1 | 4+3 | 1+0 | 12+8 | 7+7 | 3+2 |
| 12+10 | 5+2 | 12+6 | 20+1 | 12+2 | 15+5 | 13+1 |
| 14+5 | 17+8 | 8+3 | 16+3 | 10+10 | 4+4 | 12+12 |

WORDS

1. AUGUST
2. OCTOPUS
3. GRANTED
4. CARROTS

# EASY

| 11+3 | 5+5 | 12+12 | 13+5 | 10+10 | 20+1 | 1+1 |
|------|-----|-------|------|-------|------|-----|
| 7+6 | 8+4 | 11+5 | 12+1 | 6+7 | 4+4 | 21+2 |
| 5+6 | 11+11 | 14+11 | 15+3 | 14+2 | 17+2 | 16+5 |
| 10+9 | 4+2 | 9+9 | 13+2 | 6+7 | 10+6 | 1+1 |
| 4+1 | 3+3 | 11+4 | 6+1 | 4+3 | 1+0 | 15+6 |
| 10+3 | 2+2 | 11+3 | 12+6 | 6+3 | 12+5 | 6+3 |
| 10+9 | 9+4 | 1+0 | 5+4 | 11+1 | 5+4 | 4+3 |

WORDS

1. MAILING
2. PROOF
3. UPGRADE
4. BUMPS

# EASY

| | | | | | | |
|---|---|---|---|---|---|---|
| 12+12 | 4+5 | 15+10 | 5+3 | 10+10 | 11+11 | 12+14 |
| 13+11 | 4+4 | 4+1 | 11+1 | 2+0 | 10+5 | 16+7 |
| 1+1 | 3+0 | 15+4 | 12+6 | 3+2 | 1+1 | 6+7 |
| 5+5 | 12+2 | 11+4 | 1+0 | 19+2 | 12+3 | 4+5 |
| 10+11 | 10+3 | 1+0 | 10+10 | 15+3 | 18+3 | 16+2 |
| 1+0 | 11+7 | 4+3 | 5+3 | 11+7 | 19+3 | 3+1 |
| 3+3 | 5+1 | 14+6 | 8+7 | 17+4 | 19+3 | 10+11 |

WORDS

1. ARROGANCE
2. MOUTH
3. DRIBBLE
4. ARMORS

# EASY

| | | | | | | |
|---|---|---|---|---|---|---|
| 11+12 | 14+5 | 5+4 | 17+5 | 10+10 | 11+10 | 1+0 |
| 5+6 | 10+5 | 1+1 | 12+8 | 12+12 | 6+6 | 13+13 |
| 4+1 | 10+8 | 7+7 | 4+1 | 1+0 | 10+10 | 21+2 |
| 2+2 | 5+6 | 17+2 | 7+2 | 14+4 | 11+11 | 3+2 |
| 1+1 | 10+4 | 2+1 | 5+2 | 8+8 | 3+2 | 15+3 |
| 14+7 | 15+8 | 9+6 | 12+3 | 4+3 | 9+3 | 18+1 |
| 13+4 | 11+7 | 13+3 | 2+1 | 3+2 | 15+7 | 2+2 |

WORDS

1. OPERATIONS
2. ROCKER
3. VEGGIE
4. ALTERS

# EASY

| | | | | | | |
|---|---|---|---|---|---|---|
| 11+7 | 5+5 | 12+12 | 14+5 | 13+13 | 17+2 | 10+10 |
| 1+1 | 4+1 | 6+1 | 6+6 | 11+7 | 12+9 | 14+11 |
| 15+6 | 12+12 | 8+6 | 13+1 | 4+5 | 7+2 | 3+1 |
| 8+3 | 1+1 | 1+0 | 7+7 | 2+2 | 11+4 | 7+2 |
| 9+9 | 18+4 | 4+5 | 1+0 | 4+4 | 1+0 | 5+5 |
| 12+12 | 13+2 | 11+11 | 2+1 | 10+2 | 9+7 | 1+1 |
| 12+5 | 1+12 | 10+3 | 5+4 | 10+10 | 14+5 | 10+5 |

## WORDS

1. CHOIRS
2. PLANNER
3. OMITS
4. BANDAID

# EASY

| | | | | | | |
|---|---|---|---|---|---|---|
| 5+4 | 12+13 | 1+0 | 11+12 | 13+11 | 15+3 | 5+3 |
| 5+5 | 16+4 | 3+1 | 8+8 | 11+2 | 12+12 | 14+11 |
| 13+11 | 21+4 | 9+6 | 4+4 | 11+4 | 7+6 | 9+10 |
| 11+11 | 6+6 | 18+1 | 12+8 | 5+6 | 2+1 | 5+5 |
| 12+12 | 3+2 | 5+6 | 5+4 | 14+4 | 6+3 | 12+9 |
| 9+9 | 4+1 | 3+2 | 4+1 | 21+2 | 8+8 | 1+1 |
| 16+2 | 17+2 | 12+1 | 15+3 | 1+0 | 5+1 | 17+6 |

WORDS

1. COMPOSE
2. WEEKLY
3. BIRTHDAY
4. FARMERS

**EASY**

| | | | | | | |
|---|---|---|---|---|---|---|
| 1+1 | 12+11 | 10+10 | 5+6 | 17+3 | 17+9 | 11+6 |
| 6+5 | 4+1 | 10+10 | 17+2 | 5+5 | 8+4 | 9+3 |
| 15+10 | 3+2 | 14+4 | 12+3 | 12+4 | 15+3 | 6+4 |
| 3+1 | 15+8 | 3+1 | 17+2 | 10+8 | 3+3 | 18+1 |
| 12+14 | 16+3 | 1+0 | 8+7 | 7+7 | 2+1 | 16+4 |
| 13+13 | 7+5 | 14+6 | 5+4 | 8+4 | 14+7 | 2+1 |
| 16+7 | 18+4 | 3+2 | 8+6 | 10+3 | 19+4 | 5+5 |

WORDS

1. FROSTED
2. LAWYERS
3. CLIENTS
4. DONUTS

## EASY

| | | | | | | |
|---|---|---|---|---|---|---|
| 13+11 | 2+1 | 13+12 | 3+0 | 5+3 | 12+12 | 16+2 |
| 10+10 | 17+4 | 14+4 | 5+4 | 3+2 | 4+1 | 11+8 |
| 8+8 | 10+5 | 2+1 | 6+6 | 12+13 | 1+1 | 3+2 |
| 6+4 | 17+8 | 3+1 | 10+11 | 6+7 | 19+3 | 15+4 |
| 3+3 | 13+2 | 2+2 | 15+4 | 16+7 | 6+3 | 18+3 |
| 19+4 | 10+10 | 11+11 | 7+2 | 13+5 | 18+3 | 13+13 |
| 12+11 | 13+5 | 6+7 | 8+3 | 17+1 | 1+1 | 9+9 |

## WORDS

1. PORCH
2. CUCUMBER
3. RIDDLE
4. BRUISES

# EASY

| 14+5 | 6+4 | 12+7 | 12+12 | 14+6 | 13+13 | 6+4 |
|------|-----|------|-------|------|-------|-----|
| 11+12 | 1+1 | 11+2 | 21+4 | 11+11 | 15+3 | 6+9 |
| 9+4 | 3+2 | 15+4 | 11+8 | 4+1 | 10+10 | 12+12 |
| 17+2 | 13+4 | 10+10 | 14+6 | 14+10 | 11+2 | 14+1 |
| 5+6 | 4+1 | 11+8 | 1+0 | 17+3 | 7+5 | 16+2 |
| 12+5 | 11+1 | 8+8 | 7+5 | 1+0 | 18+1 | 6+5 |
| 11+12 | 21+4 | 4+1 | 1+1 | 4+4 | 10+15 | 3+2 |

## WORDS

1. STAPLES
2. LABELS
3. REMORSE
4. SYSTEM

# EASY

| | | | | | | |
|---|---|---|---|---|---|---|
| 10+11 | 14+3 | 16+5 | 17+9 | 10+10 | 11+12 | 14+5 |
| 2+1 | 10+14 | 3+3 | 4+4 | 17+6 | 14+4 | 10+10 |
| 11+4 | 14+7 | 15+10 | 18+1 | 4+3 | 14+5 | 1+1 |
| 5+4 | 15+3 | 3+2 | 1+0 | 6+6 | 5+4 | 6+7 |
| 13+11 | 12+12 | 17+2 | 10+2 | 1+0 | 4+2 | 3+2 |
| 1+1 | 5+4 | 4+1 | 12+8 | 3+3 | 3+0 | 6+4 |
| 10+9 | 10+4 | 5+3 | 1+0 | 7+7 | 9+9 | 8+7 |

## WORDS

1. FLAGS
2. ENHANCE
3. CURSE
4. TAILS

# EASY

| 16+5 | 11+11 | 4+3 | 8+6 | 13+1 | 15+4 | 10+10 |
|------|-------|------|------|------|------|-------|
| 8+7 | 11+3 | 8+7 | 12+6 | 3+2 | 9+3 | 1+1 |
| 12+13 | 13+13 | 4+5 | 7+2 | 2+2 | 6+3 | 14+10 |
| 10+4 | 6+5 | 14+8 | 14+4 | 9+7 | 11+8 | 5+5 |
| 7+6 | 13+2 | 8+1 | 6+7 | 12+1 | 1+0 | 14+5 |
| 10+10 | 4+4 | 11+2 | 1+0 | 4+2 | 9+4 | 4+1 |
| 10+10 | 7+7 | 9+7 | 12+12 | 5+3 | 2+1 | 12+8 |

## WORDS

1. EASIER
2. MOVING
3. CHAMPION
4. THIRD

**EASY**

| 14+5 | 12+1 | 6+7 | 12+12 | 13+3 | 5+3 | 10+10 |
|------|------|-----|-------|------|-----|-------|
| 9+4 | 15+4 | 11+11 | 16+2 | 18+1 | 5+4 | 4+1 |
| 1+1 | 11+8 | 12+3 | 1+0 | 6+2 | 6+6 | 13+13 |
| 15+10 | 11+4 | 15+5 | 2+1 | 4+1 | 10+10 | 3+1 |
| 10+2 | 3+2 | 11+3 | 9+9 | 6+2 | 2+2 | 11+9 |
| 5+1 | 15+6 | 12+6 | 17+3 | 1+0 | 2+1 | 18+3 |
| 2+2 | 15+3 | 3+0 | 12+2 | 10+9 | 3+3 | 12+13 |

WORDS

1. CHEATS
2. FLOORS
3. CRUNCH
4. SADDLE

## EASY

| | | | | | | |
|---|---|---|---|---|---|---|
| 12+11 | 12+7 | 5+4 | 1+1 | 5+3 | 17+3 | 19+2 |
| 10+10 | 19+2 | 13+2 | 15+5 | 12+12 | 4+1 | 11+5 |
| 11+11 | 12+5 | 17+4 | 15+3 | 7+5 | 13+2 | 13+5 |
| 12+13 | 21+2 | 5+6 | 1+0 | 2+2 | 10+10 | 7+7 |
| 14+7 | 7+5 | 10+2 | 2+1 | 1+0 | 16+8 | 9+9 |
| 4+3 | 4+1 | 1+1 | 8+7 | 2+2 | 3+2 | 12+12 |
| 13+12 | 12+2 | 5+4 | 3+1 | 9+7 | 10+11 | 14+9 |

WORDS

1. TACKLE
2. POLAR
3. SOUTHERN
4. WEDDING

**EASY**

| | | | | | | |
|---|---|---|---|---|---|---|
| 11+10 | 14+3 | 5+6 | 7+5 | 19+2 | 10+10 | 12+12 |
| 14+3 | 5+5 | 21+2 | 12+13 | 8+6 | 14+10 | 4+5 |
| 10+4 | 1+1 | 9+4 | 4+1 | 12+4 | 3+2 | 3+4 |
| 7+6 | 11+3 | 11+4 | 17+4 | 12+2 | 10+2 | 4+1 |
| 10+5 | 11+11 | 6+3 | 14+4 | 2+2 | 21+4 | 17+1 |
| 13+11 | 4+21 | 9+5 | 9+6 | 15+3 | 4+1 | 11+8 |
| 20+4 | 5+12 | 11+4 | 12+2 | 14+5 | 2+2 | 10+8 |

WORDS

1. ONIONS
2. ELDERS
3. NEWBORN
4. DRYER

**EASY**

| | | | | | | |
|---|---|---|---|---|---|---|
| 11+2 | 2+1 | 13+13 | 12+11 | 4+1 | 1+1 | 11+11 |
| 5+1 | 1+0 | 16+2 | 13+5 | 10+2 | 15+5 | 10+10 |
| 21+4 | 8+7 | 17+1 | 4+1 | 15+4 | 6+6 | 12+4 |
| 17+3 | 14+7 | 2+1 | 11+7 | 10+10 | 11+10 | 17+4 |
| 14+3 | 1+0 | 12+8 | 2+2 | 8+1 | 2+1 | 18+1 |
| 10+8 | 14+3 | 5+4 | 4+1 | 1+0 | 7+2 | 4+1 |
| 4+5 | 2+0 | 12+3 | 4+2 | 5+1 | 5+2 | 12+4 |

WORDS

1. DIFFICULT
2. ROUTE
3. CARRIAGES
4. BRACELET

# EASY

| | | | | | | |
|---|---|---|---|---|---|---|
| 5+1 | 13+12 | 11+12 | 5+2 | 4+5 | 10+0 | 19+3 |
| 18+4 | 1+0 | 7+7 | 5+5 | 11+13 | 10+10 | 14+10 |
| 2+2 | 2+1 | 5+4 | 1+0 | 5+7 | 12+12 | 18+1 |
| 13+13 | 15+8 | 5+4 | 16+3 | 3+1 | 7+2 | 3+2 |
| 3+3 | 14+11 | 9+6 | 2+2 | 12+10 | 4+3 | 12+2 |
| 14+7 | 14+2 | 1+0 | 6+6 | 2+0 | 6+1 | 5+2 |
| 15+8 | 10+6 | 19+2 | 12+2 | 15+4 | 11+10 | 10+6 |

## WORDS

1. FACIAL
2. BLOWING
3. PADDING
4. SUGGEST

# EASY

| 12+3 | 15+4 | 1+1 | 19+2 | 10+11 | 12+1 | 16+4 |
|------|------|-----|------|-------|------|------|
| 3+3 | 3+2 | 1+0 | 12+7 | 1+1 | 17+7 | 13+4 |
| 1+0 | 2+1 | 9+2 | 2+1 | 3+3 | 10+10 | 5+5 |
| 14+5 | 6+3 | 5+4 | 6+7 | 4+1 | 15+3 | 12+10 |
| 11+3 | 12+8 | 10+9 | 1+0 | 10+5 | 11+12 | 13+11 |
| 4+3 | 14+4 | 3+2 | 16+3 | 18+2 | 14+7 | 10+10 |
| 9+8 | 8+7 | 17+3 | 19+6 | 11+8 | 3+2 | 15+3 |

WORDS

1. FEATURES
2. EASTER
3. SCISSOR
4. BACKING

# EASY

| 10+10 | 12+4 | 21+3 | 2+2 | 24+1 | 1+1 | 10+11 |
|-------|------|------|------|-------|------|-------|
| 11+11 | 15+6 | 12+8 | 17+2 | 4+1 | 10+5 | 14+8 |
| 8+8 | 14+4 | 9+6 | 10+10 | 10+12 | 3+3 | 15+6 |
| 14+10 | 21+4 | 1+0 | 11+7 | 12+2 | 4+1 | 21+2 |
| 21+4 | 3+2 | 16+5 | 16+3 | 5+4 | 10+10 | 17+2 |
| 1+1 | 12+5 | 10+1 | 3+2 | 14+7 | 11+6 | 17+3 |
| 19+4 | 15+10 | 4+1 | 12+2 | 11+4 | 7+6 | 11+11 |

WORDS

1. DEFENSE
2. QUARTS
3. MONKEY
4. SQUIRT

**EASY**

| 14+10 | 19+2 | 3+4 | 12+12 | 11+13 | 24+1 | 10+10 |
|-------|------|-----|-------|-------|------|-------|
| 2+1 | 11+11 | 1+1 | 3+2 | 1+5 | 6+1 | 7+2 |
| 5+4 | 10+8 | 6+3 | 10+10 | 5+3 | 10+11 | 19+3 |
| 13+4 | 1+0 | 19+2 | 4+1 | 4+4 | 14+6 | 17+5 |
| 19+4 | 15+4 | 20+6 | 2+1 | 1+0 | 3+3 | 11+3 |
| 5+5 | 14+3 | 15+10 | 1+1 | 6+6 | 13+2 | 4+5 |
| 12+12 | 14+3 | 17+3 | 8+7 | 3+1 | 3+2 | 17+6 |

WORDS

1. BATHE
2. SUITE
3. WELCH
4. CRAZY

# EASY

| | | | | | | |
|---|---|---|---|---|---|---|
| 11+12 | 13+2 | 8+1 | 7+5 | 2+2 | 13+13 | 14+2 |
| 16+7 | 5+3 | 5+4 | 2+1 | 16+3 | 12+2 | 4+3 |
| 21+3 | 7+7 | 8+8 | 4+4 | 14+5 | 1+0 | 8+6 |
| 10+11 | 12+5 | 4+3 | 1+0 | 4+4 | 4+1 | 8+1 |
| 3+2 | 14+4 | 14+4 | 7+2 | 2+1 | 13+13 | 12+8 |
| 1+1 | 11+8 | 12+10 | 5+2 | 11+4 | 11+10 | 5+2 |
| 21+4 | 10+15 | 6+5 | 7+1 | 10+5 | 18+4 | 19+0 |

## WORDS

1. HANDLING
2. GRAPHICS
3. SERVICES
4. OUTING

## EASY

| | | | | | | |
|---|---|---|---|---|---|---|
| 15+3 | 10+10 | 19+2 | 12+3 | 12+12 | 1+0 | 16+4 |
| 13+13 | 14+5 | 4+1 | 7+3 | 5+2 | 15+8 | 13+7 |
| 10+9 | 14+6 | 8+6 | 11+11 | 10+12 | 3+2 | 11+4 |
| 14+11 | 10+5 | 11+4 | 12+13 | 6+6 | 6+2 | 15+10 |
| 5+4 | 4+5 | 6+7 | 16+3 | 2+1 | 13+2 | 10+2 |
| 5+1 | 2+1 | 5+3 | 1+0 | 19+4 | 23+2 | 10+10 |
| 14+10 | 8+7 | 11+8 | 9+5 | 14+5 | 11+12 | 1+1 |

WORDS

1. TWELVE
2. STOMACH
3. TOYOTA
4. SCION

# EASY

| | | | | | | |
|---|---|---|---|---|---|---|
| 15+4 | 11+12 | 6+5 | 10+10 | 19+3 | 12+12 | 14+11 |
| 1+1 | 3+2 | 12+12 | 4+5 | 10+10 | 10+4 | 5+5 |
| 8+8 | 15+7 | 23+3 | 12+2 | 6+1 | 4+1 | 8+1 |
| 9+10 | 7+2 | 3+2 | 1+0 | 16+2 | 5+0 | 6+2 |
| 10+3 | 10+4 | 3+13 | 4+3 | 9+5 | 14+7 | 15+4 |
| 4+1 | 3+2 | 2+1 | 1+0 | 15+5 | 14+4 | 3+2 |
| 16+7 | 2+2 | 18+3 | 1+0 | 12+1 | 18+1 | 9+7 |

WORDS

1. SEVENTEEN
2. MAGAZINE
3. DECATUR
4. PERSHING

# EASY

| 12+12 | 4+5 | 1+1 | 17+2 | 10+10 | 11+12 | 13+1 |
|-------|-----|-----|------|-------|-------|------|
| 18+1 | 10+5 | 10+10 | 9+12 | 3+2 | 4+1 | 12+12 |
| 5+12 | 14+7 | 4+1 | 18+4 | 17+4 | 7+5 | 18+2 |
| 22+3 | 6+6 | 3+2 | 3+2 | 12+13 | 21+4 | 11+8 |
| 13+5 | 15+4 | 4+1 | 14+4 | 3+1 | 10+9 | 13+7 |
| 11+12 | 15+7 | 16+6 | 14+4 | 12+8 | 18+1 | 1+1 |
| 5+5 | 1+0 | 1+0 | 4+1 | 10+9 | 7+2 | 4+6 |

WORDS

1. STREETS
2. BOULEVARD
3. SLEEVES
4. WAVES

# ANSWERS

| | | | | | | |
|---|---|---|---|---|---|---|
| | | 12+11=W (4) | | | | |
| | | | 1+0=A (4) | | | |
| | | 9+11=T (4) | | | 2+1=C (2) | 16+2=R (3) |
| | 3+2=E (4) | 3+3=F (1) | | 10+5=O (2) | | 4+1=E (3) |
| 13+6=S (4) | 9+9=R (4) | | 1+0=A (1) | 11+7=R (2) | 4+3=G (3) | |
| | 5+3=H (1) | 4+5=I (1) | 12+8=T (2) | 7+7=N (3) | 14+4=R (2) | |
| | 10+10=T (1) | 1+1=B (3) | 1+0=A (3) | 1+2=C (2) | 3+2=E (2) | |

| | | | | | | |
|---|---|---|---|---|---|---|
| | | | 12+6=R (2) | 17+2=S (2) | | 1+0=A (1) |
| 1+0=A (4) | | 8+7=O (2) | 5+2=G (3) | 12+2=N (3) | 2+1=C (1) | |
| 2+2=D (4) | 15+3=R (2) | 12+8=T (1) | 8+8=P (1) | 5+4=I (3) | 2+1=C (1) | |
| | 3+1=D (4) | 10+8=R (2) | 5+6=K (3) | 3+2=E (1) | | |
| | 7+2=I (4) | 6+6=L (3) | 6+3=I (2) | | | |
| 13+7=T (4) | 1+0=A (3) | 10+5=O (4) | | 6+7=M (2) | | |
| | 7+2=I (4) | 15+8=W (3) | 8+6=N (4) | | | |

| | | | | | | | |
|---|---|---|---|---|---|---|---|
| 2+1=C (3) | | 2+2=D (1) | 14+7=U (2) | 6+6=L (2) | | | |
| 4+4=H (3) | | 8+8=P (2) | 3+2=E (1) | | 1+0=A (2) | | |
| | 1+0=A (3) | 16+7=W (1) | 4+5=I (2) | 3+2=E (4) | | 15+5=T (2) | |
| | 12+2=N (3) | 4+1=E (1) | 10+2=L (4) | 7+7=N (2) | 3+1=D (4) | 4+1=E (2) | |
| | 13+1=N (1) | 4+3=G (3) | 7+5=L (4) | 1+0=A (2) | | | |
| | 3+2=E (1) | 10+9=S (3) | 4+1=E (3) | 3+2=E (4) | 8+5=M (2) | | |
| | | 10+8=R (1) | | | 15+10=Y (4) | | |

| | | | | | | |
|---|---|---|---|---|---|---|
| | 16+2=R (1) | 11+8=S (1) | | | | |
| | 3+2=E (1) | 10+9=S (2) | | | | |
| 5+2=G (4) | 3+2=E (2) | 2+2=D (1) | 14+5=S (2) | | | 4+3=G (3) |
| 12+2=N (4) | 10+8=R (2) | | 15+3=R (1) | | 15+3=R (3) | |
| 7+2=I (4) | 7+8=O (4) | 12+8=T (2) | 14+7=U (1) | 3+2=E (3) | | |
| 13+13=Z (4) | 11+3=N (4) | 11+2=M (1) | 6+3=I (2) | 3+2=E (3) | 21+2=W (2) | |
| | | | 10+4=N (3) | 1+0=A (2) | | |

**PAGE 11**

| | | | | | | |
|---|---|---|---|---|---|---|
| 10+6=P (1) | 3+2=E (1) | | | | | |
| 1+0=A (1) | 4+4=H (2) | 12+6=R (1) | 18+1=S (1) | | 17+4=U (4) | |
| 2+1=C (2) | 14+2=P (1) | | | 12+2=N (4) | | |
| | 1+0=A (2) | 3+2=E (2) | | 5+4=I (4) | | |
| | 1+0=A (3) | 11+7=R (2) | 2+1=C (4) | 9+6=O (4) | 6+3=I (3) | 8+6=N (4) |
| | 7+7=N (3) | 1+0=A (3) | 2+0=B (2) | 10+4=N (3) | 15+3=R (4) | |
| | | | 6+3=I (3) | 2+2=D (3) | | |

**PAGE 12**

| | | | | | | |
|---|---|---|---|---|---|---|
| | 12+7=S (4) | | | | | |
| | 10+6=P (4) | | | | | |
| | 11+4=O (4) | 3+2=E (1) | 17+3=T (1) | | 10+5=O (2) | 4+4=H (2) |
| 12+6=R (4) | 5+6=K (1) | 20+5=Y (2) | 11+8=S (3) | 1+1=B (1) | 2+1=C (2) | |
| 12+8=T (4) | 10+9=S (1) | 10+3=M (3) | 3+2=E (2) | 9+2=K (2) | 1+0=A (1) | |
| | 15+4=S (4) | 1+0=A (1) | 1+0=A (3) | 6+6=L (1) | | |
| | | 2+0=B (1) | 8+4=L (1) | 4+1=E (3) | 10+10=T (3) | |

PAGE 13

| | | | | | | | |
|---|---|---|---|---|---|---|---|
| | | | 22+3=Y (1) | | | | |
| | | 18+2=T (1) | 4+1=E (3) | 16+2=R (4) | 19+0=S (4) | | |
| | 4+5=I (1) | 3+1=D (3) | 3+2=E (4) | 12+6=R (3) | | | |
| 12+2=N (1) | | 15+5=T (4) | | 1+0=A (3) | 11+9=T (2) | | |
| 1+0=A (1) | 10+2=L (4) | 10+4=N (1) | | 7+2=I (2) | 14+7=U (3) | 12+7=S (2) | |
| | 14+5=S (1) | 7+2=I (4) | 6+3=I (1) | 6+7=M (2) | 3+2=E (2) | 14+3=Q (3) | |
| | | | 4+2=F (4) | | | 10+9=S (3) | |

PAGE 14

| | | | | | | |
|---|---|---|---|---|---|---|
| 10+8=R (1) | | | 6+2=H (2) | | | |
| 3+2=E (1) | 2+2=D (1) | 9+6=O (3) | 5+6=K (3) | 2+1=C (2) | | 15+4=S (4) |
| 7+7=N (1) | 11+4=O (3) | 11+1=L (1) | | 1+0=A (2) | 2+1=C (1) | 10+8=R (4) |
| | 7+5=L (3) | | 7+2=I (1) | 5+3=H (1) | 3+2=E (2) | 4+1=E (4) |
| | 10+10=T (3) | | | 12+2=N (4) | 2+2=D (4) | 8+4=L (2) |
| | | 17+4=U (3) | 11+4=O (4) | | 1+1=B (2) | |
| | | 11+4=O (3) | | 16+7=W (4) | | |

| | | | | | | | |
|---|---|---|---|---|---|---|---|
| | | | | 11+2=M (4) | | | |
| | | | | | 4+1=E (4) | | 10+9=S (3) |
| 3+3=F (1) | | 14+11=Y (4) | | | 17+2=S (4) | 2+1=C (3) | |
| 8+7=O (1) | | 2+3=E (2) | 11+8=S (4) | | | 16+2=R (3) | |
| | 12+12=X (1) | 12+6=R (2) | 3+2=E (3) | 1+0=A (2) | 1+0=A (3) | | |
| | 5+4=I (2) | 4+1=E (1) | 3+1=D (2) | 11+1=L (3) | 1+1=B (3) | | |
| | 15+4=S (1) | 10+3=M (2) | | 1+1=B (3) | | | |

| | | | | | | |
|---|---|---|---|---|---|---|
| 4+1=E (3) | 2+1=C (1) | | | 14+5=S (4) | | |
| 2+3=E (1) | 10+6=P (3) | 18+3=U (1) | | | 11+7=R (4) | |
| 10+2=L (1) | 8+7=O (3) | 2+2=D (1) | | 11+4=O (4) | 4+1=E (3) | |
| 14+4=R (2) | 2+2=D (1) | 6+6=L (3) | | 5+4=I (4) | 11+3=N (3) | |
| | 2+3=E (2) | 14+1=O (2) | 3+2=E (3) | 11+11=V (3) | 8+6=N (4) | |
| | 9+7=P (2) | | 15+3=R (2) | 8+8=P (2) | 4+1=E (4) | |
| | | | | | | 12+7=S (4) |

**PAGE 17**

|  |  |  | 16+3=S (2) |  | 10+9=S (1) |  |
|---|---|---|---|---|---|---|
|  |  | 10+1=K (2) |  |  | 1+0=A (1) |  |
|  | 2+1=C (2) |  | 4+1=E (1) | 15+6=U (1) |  |  |
|  | 5+4=I (2) | 3+2=E (4) | 4+1=E (4) | 2+1=C (1) |  |  |
| 17+2=S (3) |  | 10+4=N (2) | 2+1=C (3) | 10+8=R (4) | 1+0=A (3) | 5+1=F (3) |
|  | 7+7=N (3) | 10+5=O (3) | 7+4=K (2) | 10+2=L (3) | 4+4=H (4) |  |
|  |  |  |  |  | 14+6=T (4) |  |

**PAGE 18**

|  |  | 11+7=R (3) |  | 4+1=E (2) |  |  |
|---|---|---|---|---|---|---|
|  | 4+1=E (3) |  | 11+1=L (2) | 4+3=G (1) |  |  |
|  | 12+8=T (3) | 15+5=T (2) | 1+0=A (1) | 15+5=T (4) | 11+4=O (1) |  |
|  | 4+4=H (3) | 2+1=C (1) | 12+8=T (2) | 11+4=O (4) |  | 17+2=S (4) |
|  | 7+2=I (3) | 5+4=I (1) | 1+0=A (2) | 3+2=E (2) | 8+7=O (4) | 4+4=H (4) |
| 2+1=C (1) | 4+4=H (1) | 10+4=N (3) |  |  | 16+3=S (2) |  |
|  |  |  | 7+4=K (3) |  |  |  |

| | | | | | | |
|---|---|---|---|---|---|---|
| | | | | | | |
| | | 5+4=I (3) | 12+2=N (1) | 10+10=T (1) | | |
| | 7+5=L (3) | 3+2=E (1) | 13+1=N (3) | | 15+4=S (3) | |
| | | | 2+1=C (1) | 10+1=K (3) | | |
| | | 5+6=K (2) | 5+5=J (1) | 1+0=A (1) | | 9+4=M (4) |
| 4+3=G (4) | 1+0=A (1) | 2+2=D (1) | 1+0=A (2) | 3+2=E (2) | 13+2=O (4) | |
| | 12+2=N (4) | 7+2=I (4) | 7+7=N (4) | 14+4=R (4) | 12+11=W (2) | |

| | | | | | | |
|---|---|---|---|---|---|---|
| | | | | 3+2=E (4) | 7+5=L (4) | 14+6=T (4) |
| | 8+8=P (1) | 9+6=O (2) | 10+3=M (2) | | 10+10=T (4) | |
| | 10+9=S (2) | 1+0=A (1) | | 3+2=E (2) | 4+1=E (1) | 3+2=E (4) |
| | 3+2=E (2) | 2+2=D (1) | | 10+2=L (1) | | 8+3=K (4) |
| 13+5=R (2) | | | 3+1=D (1) | | | |
| | 5+4=I (2) | 11+1=L (3) | | 12+8=T (3) | 17+2=S (3) | |
| | 4+1=E (3) | 16+4=T (2) | 22+3=Y (3) | | | |

| | | | | | | |
|---|---|---|---|---|---|---|
| | | | | 4+3=G (3) | | |
| 2+1=C (1) | | | 1+0=A (3) | | | |
| | 10+8=R (1) | 15+5=T (3) | | | | 10+9=S (2) |
| | 1+0=A (1) | 3+2=E (3) | | 4+1=E (1) | | 3+2=E (2) |
| | 2+2=D (3) | 2+2=D (1) | 6+6=L (1) | 12+2=N (4) | 15+7=V (2) | |
| | 6+3=I (4) | 7+7=N (4) | 3+2=E (4) | | 7+2=I (2) | |
| | | 11+1=L (4) | | 11+12=W (2) | | |

| | | | | | | | |
|---|---|---|---|---|---|---|---|
| | | | | 18+1=S (4) | 17+1=R (4) | | |
| | | | 5+2=G (1) | 5+4=I (2) | 6+7=M (2) | 3+2=E (4) | |
| | 10+9=S (3) | 10+2=L (2) | 12+8=T (2) | 6+3=I (1) | 5+2=G (4) | 1+0=A (2) | |
| 3+2=E (3) | 16+5=U (2) | | | 12+6=R (1) | 11+4=O (4) | 18+2=T (2) | |
| 14+4=R (3) | | | 8+4=L (1) | 15+3=R (4) | 4+1=E (2) | | |
| | 8+7=O (3) | | 15+4=S (1) | | 6+5=K (4) | | |
| | | 10+10=T (3) | 17+2=S (3) | | | | |

| | | | | | | | |
|---|---|---|---|---|---|---|---|
| | 17+3=T (2) | | 10+9=S (1) | | 14+5=S (4) | | |
| 14+4=R (2) | | 6+6=L (2) | | 12+2=N (1) | 12+8=T (3) | 4+3=G (4) | |
| 1+0=A (2) | 7+2=I (2) | | 6+7=M (3) | 5+4=I (3) | 14+1=O (1) | 8+6=N (4) | |
| | 10+12=V (1) | 3+2=E (1) | 10+3=M (3) | | 6+3=I (1) | 5+4=I (4) | |
| | | 12+3=O (3) | 11+7=R (1) | 15+4=S (1) | 14+4=R (4) | | |
| | | 2+1=C (3) | | | 12+8=T (4) | 17+2=S (4) | |

| | | | | | | | |
|---|---|---|---|---|---|---|---|
| | | 16+2=R (2) | 9+3=L (4) | | | | 2+1=C (4) |
| | | 3+2=E (2) | 4+1=E (4) | 6+6=L (4) | 10+5=O (4) | | |
| | 10+3=M (2) | 4+3=G (4) | 11+8=S (1) | 12+7=S (4) | | | |
| | 4+3=G (1) | 11+4=O (2) | 3+2=E (4) | 12+8=T (1) | | | |
| | 2+3=E (1) | 12+2=N (1) | 15+5=T (2) | 14+4=R (1) | | 6+4=J (3) | |
| 14+4=R (1) | 21+4=Y (3) | 3+2=E (2) | 1+0=A (1) | | 4+1=E (3) | | |
| | | 4+1=E (3) | 16+3=S (3) | 13+5=R (3) | | | |

**PAGE 25**

| | | | | | | |
|---|---|---|---|---|---|---|
| | | 1+0=A (2) | | 17+1=R (3) | 17+2=S (4) | |
| 8+6=N (1) | | | 3+1=D (2) | | 3+2=E (3) | 15+3=R (4) |
| | 8+7=O (1) | 5+4=I (2) | 10+6=P (1) | 15+7=V (3) | | 4+1=E (4) |
| | 11+7=R (2) | 17+3=T (1) | 3+2=E (3) | 8+5=M (1) | 7+6=M (4) | |
| | 11+4=O (2) | | 15+5=T (3) | 11+2=M (4) | 14+1=O (1) | |
| | | 7+5=L (2) | 7+2=I (4) | 1+0=A (3) | 1+2=C (1) | |
| | 12+7=S (4) | 11+12=W (4) | 4+2=F (2) | | 4+4=H (3) | 19+4=W (3) |

**PAGE 26**

| | | | | | | |
|---|---|---|---|---|---|---|
| | | 10+8=R (3) | 16+3=S (3) | | | |
| 10+2=L (2) | 4+1=E (3) | 1+0=A (1) | 1+0=A (4) | | | |
| 15+7=V (3) | 3+2=E (2) | 3+1=D (4) | 1+1=B (1) | 3+2=E (4) | | |
| 6+3=I (3) | 8+6=N (2) | 15+6=U (1) | | 4+4=H (4) | | |
| 2+2=D (3) | 2+1=C (1) | 7+7=N (2) | 14+7=U (2) | 10+8=R (4) | 4+1=E (4) | |
| | | 15+4=S (1) | | 10+10=T (2) | | 11+11=V (4) |
| | | | | | | 8+7=O (4) |

|  |  |  | 10+10=T (3) |  |  |  |
|---|---|---|---|---|---|---|
| 5+2=G (4) |  | 17+2=S (2) |  | 2+1=C (3) | 4+3=G (1) |  |
|  | 11+3=N (4) |  | 2+2=D (2) | 12+2=N (1) | 4+1=E (3) |  |
|  | 7+2=I (4) | 8+8=P (1) | 8+6=N (2) | 3+3=F (3) | 5+4=I (1) |  |
| 14+6=T (4) | 15+4=S (1) | 14+7=U (2) | 3+2=E (1) | 10+8=R (3) | 6+6=L (1) |  |
| 10+9=S (4) | 14+1=O (2) | 21+2=W (4) |  | 10+2=L (1) | 3+2=E (3) | 9+7=P (3) |
|  | 7+2=I (4) | 11+5=P (2) | 15+5=T (4) |  |  |  |

|  |  |  |  |  | 11+8=S (1) |  |
|---|---|---|---|---|---|---|
|  |  | 8+5=M (1) | 3+2=E (1) | 12+2=N (2) | 10+10=T (1) | 3+2=E (2) |
|  | 17+4=U (1) |  | 1+0=A (2) | 10+4=N (1) | 4+3=G (2) |  |
| 2+1=C (1) |  | 5+3=H (2) | 5+4=I (3) | 12+2=N (3) | 3+2=E (4) |  |
|  | 10+5=O (1) | 8+8=P (3) | 2+1=C (2) | 14+10=X (2) | 5+2=G (3) | 10+9=S (4) |
|  | 11+5=P (3) | 2+2=D (1) | 3+0=C (4) | 15+3=R (4) | 4+1=E (2) | 6+3=I (4) |
|  |  | 6+3=I (3) | 4+4=H (3) | 13+6=S (3) | 19+2=U (4) |  |

| | | | | | | |
|---|---|---|---|---|---|---|
| | 14+6=T (4) | | | | | |
| | | 1+0=A (4) | 3+2=E (4) | | | |
| | 1+1=B (4) | 8+4=L (4) | 15+5=T (2) | 14+4=R (1) | 14+4=R (2) | |
| | | 2+1=C (2) | 14+7=U (1) | 8+7=O (2) | 6+5=K (1) | 23+2=Y (2) |
| | 4+1=E (2) | 12+8=T (1) | | 3+2=E (1) | 1+0=A (3) | |
| | 12+6=R (2) | 3+2=E (3) | 12+8=T (3) | 16+3=S (3) | 20+5=Y (1) | 9+6=O (3) |
| 16+3=S (3) | 16+2=R (3) | 6+3=I (2) | 3+1=D (2) | | 1+2=C (3) | |

| | | | | | | |
|---|---|---|---|---|---|---|
| 1+2=C (3) | | 8+8=P (3) | 15+5=T (3) | 4+3=G (2) | | |
| | 1+0=A (3) | | 7+7=N (2) | 1+0=A (3) | 10+10=T (1) | |
| | | 5+4=I (2) | 4+1=E (1) | 12+2=N (1) | 6+3=I (3) | |
| | 10+6=P (2) | 12+7=S (1) | | | 10+4=N (3) | |
| | 4+1=E (1) | 14+4=R (2) | 7+2=I (2) | 4+4=H (2) | | 16+3=S (3) |
| 10+2=L (4) | 10+8=R (1) | 11+11=V (4) | 13+5=R (4) | | 2+1=C (2) | |
| | 3+2=E (4) | 14+2=P (1) | | 1+0=A (4) | 6+7=M (4) | |

| | | | | | | |
|---|---|---|---|---|---|---|
| 3+2=E (3) | | 14+5=S (1) | 10+8=R (1) | | | |
| | 15+7=V (3) | | | 3+2=E (1) | | |
| | 3+2=E (3) | 14+4=R (3) | 12+13=Y (1) | | 8+7=O (3) | |
| | | 1+0=A (1) | 21+4=Y (3) | 1+1=B (3) | 2+1=C (2) | 2+2=D (3) |
| | | 7+5=L (1) | 4+3=G (4) | 10+8=R (4) | 9+6=O (2) | 19+6=Y (3) |
| | 11+7=R (2) | 15+10=Y (2) | 11+5=P (1) | 14+7=U (2) | 4+1=E (4) | |
| | | 12+8=T (2) | 8+6=N (2) | | 12+8=T (4) | 1+0=A (4) |

| | | | | | | |
|---|---|---|---|---|---|---|
| | 6+3=I (3) | 12+2=N (3) | 5+2=G (3) | 2+2=D (2) | | |
| | | 15+7=V (3) | | | 3+2=E (2) | 13+5=R (4) |
| | 1+0=A (3) | | 3+2=E (1) | | 11+8=S (2) | 3+2=E (4) |
| 5+3=H (3) | | 15+5=T (1) | | | 6+5=K (2) | 2+1=C (4) |
| | 1+0=A (1) | 4+1=E (4) | 17+5=V (4) | 10+3=M (1) | 4+1=E (4) | 12+8=T (2) |
| | 20+2=V (1) | | 11+4=O (1) | 5+4=I (4) | | 10+5=O (2) |
| | | 5+4=I (1) | 16+4=T (1) | | 8+8=P (2) | |

| | | | | | | |
|---|---|---|---|---|---|---|
| | 2+1=C (2) | | | 12+3=O (3) | 13+1=N (3) | |
| | 7+4=K (2) | 17+4=U (2) | 5+4=I (3) | | 9+2=K (2) | |
| 21+4=Y (2) | 14+5=S (4) | 10+10=T (3) | 15+5=T (2) | | 4+1=E (2) | |
| | 12+1=M (4) | 12+8=T (1) | 19+2=U (3) | 7+7=N (2) | | |
| | 14+7=U (1) | 14+4=R (4) | 2+1=C (3) | 17+3=T (1) | | |
| | 8+7=O (1) | 12+3=O (4) | 5+4=I (1) | 3+2=E (3) | | |
| | 4+2=F (4) | 4+1=E (1) | 7+6=M (1) | | 12+12=X (3) | 3+2=E (3) |

| | | | | | | | |
|---|---|---|---|---|---|---|---|
| | | | 14+6=T (4) | 5+4=I (4) | | | |
| | 4+1=E (1) | 15+7=V (1) | 17+2=S (3) | 1+0=A (4) | | | 1+0=A (4) |
| 13+5=R (1) | | 3+2=E (3) | 10+5=O (1) | | 15+8=W (4) | | |
| | | 8+6=N (1) | 4+4=H (3) | 16+2=R (2) | 13+2=O (2) | | |
| | | 10+8=R (1) | 3+2=E (2) | 17+2=S (3) | | | 2+1=C (2) |
| | | 16+3=S (2) | 14+7=U (1) | 15+5=T (1) | 6+3=I (3) | | 11+8=S (2) |
| | | | | | 10+13=W (3) | | |

## PAGE 35

| | | | | | | |
|---|---|---|---|---|---|---|
| | 15+3=R (4) | 14+7=U (4) | 2+0=B (4) | 7+5=L (4) | | |
| | 8+8=P (4) | 3+2=E (4) | 5+3=H (2) | 5+4=I (4) | 12+2=N (1) | |
| | | 14+6=T (2) | 21+4=Y (3) | 1+0=A (1) | 2+1=C (4) | 12+8=T (1) |
| | 7+7=N (2) | | 6+6=L (3) | 5+2=G (1) | 6+3=I (1) | |
| 4+1=E (2) | | 4+3=G (1) | 5+4=I (1) | 10+4=N (3) | 2+1=C (1) | |
| | 11+11=V (2) | | 6+3=I (3) | 1+0=A (3) | | |
| | | 4+1=E (2) | 11+8=S (2) | | 11+2=M (3) | |

## PAGE 36

| | | | | | | | |
|---|---|---|---|---|---|---|---|
| | | | | | 5+2=G (4) | 12+2=N (4) | |
| | 9+5=N (2) | | | | | 16+3=S (3) | 5+4=I (4) |
| | | 17+4=U (2) | 10+3=M (2) | 4+1=E (3) | | | 8+4=L (4) |
| | | 1+0=A (3) | 14+4=R (3) | 1+1=B (2) | 10+2=L (4) | 12+7=S (1) | |
| | 7+5=L (3) | 2+2=D (1) | 14+4=R (2) | 3+2=E (2) | 12+3=O (1) | 1+0=A (4) | |
| 3+3=F (3) | | | 10+5=O (1) | | 12+2=N (1) | 1+1=B (4) | |
| | | | 6+7=M (1) | 5+4=I (1) | | | |

| | | | | | | |
|---|---|---|---|---|---|---|
| | | 15+4=S (3) | 17+2=S (3) | | | |
| | 2+0=B (2) | 4+1=E (3) | | | 2+1=C (1) | |
| | | 18+3=U (2) | 12+2=N (3) | | 10+5=O (1) | |
| | | 14+6=T (2) | 5+4=I (3) | 21+1=V (1) | | 17+2=S (2) |
| 15+4=S (4) | 12+4=P (3) | 9+7=P (3) | 10+10=T (2) | 3+2=E (1) | 8+6=N (2) | |
| 4+1=E (4) | 1+0=A (3) | 7+2=I (4) | 4+1=E (1) | 8+7=O (2) | 12+6=R (1) | |
| | 18+2=T (4) | 6+2=H (3) | 5+6=K (4) | 5+2=G (1) | 1+0=A (1) | |

**PAGE 38**

| | | | | | | |
|---|---|---|---|---|---|---|
| | | | | | | |
| | 15+4=S (2) | | 4+1=E (3) | 11+12=W (2) | 1+0=A (2) | |
| | | 13+7=T (2) | 14+7=U (2) | 12+8=T (3) | 7+5=L (2) | |
| | | 6+6=L (1) | 1+0=A (3) | 7+7=N (2) | | |
| | 8+7=O (3) | 11+1=L (3) | 5+4=I (1) | | 11+8=S (4) | 4+3=G (1) |
| 16+3=S (3) | | 9+3=L (4) | 20+2=V (1) | 16+3=S (4) | 8+6=N (1) | 3+2=E (4) |
| 7+2=I (3) | 6+1=G (4) | | 1+0=A (4) | 6+3=I (1) | | 18+1=S (4) |

| | | | 10+9=S (2) | | | |
|---|---|---|---|---|---|---|
| | | 12+6=R (4) | | 4+4=H (2) | | |
| | | 15+4=S (4) | 8+7=O (4) | 3+2=E (2) | | |
| 10+9=S (4) | 3+2=E (4) | 16+4=T (2) | 4+1=E (2) | 2+2=D (3) | 13+5=R (3) | |
| | 12+7=S (2) | 21+4=Y (1) | 3+2=E (3) | | 8+8=P (1) | 1+0=A (3) |
| | | 11+9=T (1) | 16+2=R (3) | 14+4=R (1) | | 9+6=O (3) |
| | | | 15+5=T (1) | 3+2=E (1) | 1+1=B (3) | |

| | | 7+2=I (3) | 4+3=G (3) | 17+2=S (4) | | |
|---|---|---|---|---|---|---|
| | 13+9=V (3) | 4+1=E (1) | 9+3=L (4) | 17+1=R (3) | | |
| 2+3=E (3) | 6+6=L (1) | 10+2=L (2) | 1+0=A (4) | 13+2=O (3) | | 1+0=A (4) |
| 10+4=N (3) | 1+0=A (2) | 13+3=P (1) | | 11+2=M (4) | 5+1=F (3) | 12+2=N (4) |
| | 4+1=E (2) | 5+4=I (1) | | | 7+2=I (4) | |
| | 14+4=R (1) | 6+7=M (2) | | 1+0=A (2) | 12+3=O (2) | |
| 10+10=T (1) | | | 15+5=T (2) | | | |

| | | | | | | |
|---|---|---|---|---|---|---|
| | 3+3=F (1) | | 18+1=S (4) | 3+2=E (4) | | |
| | 11+3=N (2) | 10+5=O (1) | | | 14+5=S (4) | 2+1=C (4) |
| | 3+2=E (2) | 13+8=U (1) | | 12+7=S (4) | 5+3=H (1) | 15+3=R (4) |
| 7+7=N (3) | | 14+6=T (2) | 10+8=R (1) | 12+8=T (1) | 9+6=O (4) | |
| | 11+4=O (3) | 10+10=T (2) | | | | |
| | 2+2=D (3) | 5+4=I (2) | 1+0=A (3) | 1+1=B (3) | 1+0=A (3) | |
| | | 12+2=N (3) | 10+3=M (2) | | | |

**PAGE 42**

| | | | | | | |
|---|---|---|---|---|---|---|
| | | 12+8=T (3) | | | 10+9=S (1) | |
| | 1+0=A (3) | 11+8=S (2) | 4+1=E (3) | | | 3+2=E (1) |
| | 8+6=N (3) | 5+6=K (2) | | | 12+7=S (1) | |
| | 2+1=C (2) | 5+4=I (3) | | 1+0=A (1) | | |
| | 8+7=O (2) | 10+3=M (3) | 12+10=V (1) | | | |
| | 1+0=A (3) | 17+2=S (2) | | 6+7=M (4) | | |
| 7+5=L (3) | 6+6=L (4) | 7+2=I (4) | 1+0=A (4) | | 3+2=E (4) | |

| | | | | | | | |
|---|---|---|---|---|---|---|---|
| | 7+7=N (1) | | | | | | |
| 4+3=G (1) | 5+4=I (1) | | | | | | |
| | 4+1=E (3) | 3+2=E (1) | | 14+4=R (3) | 7+2=I (4) | 11+2=M (4) | |
| 10+8=R (3) | 12+1=M (3) | 15+3=R (1) | 3+2=E (3) | 6+6=L (4) | 2+2=D (3) | | |
| 16+3=S (3) | 11+4=O (1) | 1+0=A (3) | | | 3+2=E (4) | | |
| 11+8=S (2) | | 4+2=F (1) | 14+7=U (2) | 4+3=G (4) | 1+0=A (4) | | |
| | 5+1=F (2) | 3+3=F (2) | 4+1=E (4) | 2+1=C (2) | | | |

| | | | | | | | |
|---|---|---|---|---|---|---|---|
| | | | | 2+1=C (4) | 4+4=H (4) | 10+2=L (3) | |
| | 9+4=M (2) | 1+0=A (4) | | | 3+2=E (3) | 8+6=N (1) | |
| 3+2=E (2) | 12+3=O (4) | | | 15+7=V (3) | 9+6=O (1) | | |
| | 10+9=S (2) | 11+7=R (4) | | 12+8=T (1) | 1+0=A (3) | | 10+8=R (2) |
| | 16+3=S (2) | 13+6=S (1) | | 12+2=N (2) | 12+6=R (3) | 4+1=E (2) | |
| | | 3+2=E (2) | | 13+2=O (1) | 5+2=G (2) | 15+5=T (3) | |
| | | | | 1+1=B (1) | | | |

**PAGE 45**

| | | | | | | |
|---|---|---|---|---|---|---|
| | | 2+2=D (4) | | | 2+1=C (4) | |
| | | | 12+11=W (4) | | 11+7=R (4) | |
| 16+4=T (2) | | 14+4=R (1) | | 13+2=O (4) | 18+4=V (2) | 4+1=E (3) |
| | 7+7=N (2) | 2+3=E (1) | | 10+8=R (2) | 3+2=E (2) | 2+1=C (3) |
| | 5+3=H (1) | 8+7=O (2) | 6+7=M (2) | 4+2=F (1) | 5+4=I (3) | |
| | | 14+6=T (1) | 1+0=A (1) | | 17+3=T (3) | |
| | | | | 11+4=O (3) | 10+4=N (3) | |

**PAGE 46**

| | | | | | | |
|---|---|---|---|---|---|---|
| | | 15+6=U (4) | 11+7=R (4) | 15+5=T (4) | | |
| | | 10+5=O (1) | 14+2=P (4) | 5+6=K (4) | | |
| | 6+6=L (1) | 4+3=G (2) | 8+8=P (1) | 8+6=N (4) | 10+10=T (1) | |
| 7+2=I (1) | | 7+7=N (2) | 10+3=M (1) | 1+0=A (4) | 11+7=R (1) | 17+2=S (3) |
| | 12+2=N (1) | | 6+3=I (2) | 1+0=A (1) | 1+1=B (4) | 15+8=W (3) |
| | | 3+2=E (1) | 1+1=B (2) | 7+5=L (3) | 11+4=O (3) | |
| | 12+11=W (3) | 5+4=I (3) | 10+2=L (3) | 14+7=U (2) | 11+9=T (2) | |

| | | | | | | |
|---|---|---|---|---|---|---|
| | | | | | 4+1=E (4) | |
| | 3+2=E (1) | | 13+5=R (1) | | 17+5=V (4) | |
| | 2+1=C (2) | 12+10=V (1) | | 3+2=E (1) | | 4+1=E (4) |
| 8+7=O (2) | | 3+2=E (2) | 8+6=N (2) | | 16+3=S (1) | 5+4=I (4) |
| | 13+1=N (2) | | | 10+10=T (2) | 1+1=B (1) | 7+5=L (4) |
| | 16+3=S (3) | 10+4=N (2) | 11+1=L (3) | | 4+1=E (4) | 11+4=O (1) |
| | | 3+2=E (3) | 5+4=I (2) | 1+0=A (3) | 16+4=T (3) | 1+1=B (4) |

| | | | | | | |
|---|---|---|---|---|---|---|
| | | | | | | |
| | | 1+1=B (2) | | 1+0=A (1) | | 16+2=R (4) |
| | 1+0=A (2) | | 8+8=P (1) | 5+3=H (3) | 14+6=T (1) | 4+1=E (4) |
| 2+2=D (2) | | 18+3=U (1) | 12+8=T (3) | 6+3=I (1) | 11+5=P (4) | |
| | 7+5=L (2) | 3+0=C (1) | 1+0=A (3) | 10+3=M (4) | 12+3=O (1) | |
| | 15+10=Y (2) | 4+1=E (3) | 2+1=C (1) | 7+7=N (1) | 1+0=A (4) | |
| | 5+3=H (3) | | 10+5=O (1) | | | 1+2=C (4) |

**PAGE 49**

| | | | | | | | |
|---|---|---|---|---|---|---|---|
| | | | 14+5=S (1) | | | | |
| | 2+2=D (4) | 14+4=R (1) | | 5+2=G (3) | | | |
| | 3+2=E (1) | 1+0=A (4) | 3+1=D (4) | 10+4=N (3) | | | 17+2=S (4) |
| 5+2=G (2) | | 17+8=Y (1) | 6+3=I (3) | 2+2=D (4) | 1+0=A (2) | 4+1=E (4) | |
| | 12+2=N (2) | 5+2=G (3) | 1+0=A (1) | 8+6=N (2) | 6+3=I (4) | | |
| 6+2=H (3) | 6+3=I (2) | 4+3=G (3) | 11+7=R (1) | 20+5=Y (2) | | | |
| | 15+6=U (3) | 4+4=H (2) | 10+10=T (2) | 10+6=P (1) | | | |

**PAGE 50**

| | | | | | | | |
|---|---|---|---|---|---|---|---|
| | | 3+2=E (1) | 17+2=S (1) | 12+2=N (3) | | | |
| | 4+3=G (1) | 16+3=S (4) | 4+3=G (3) | 17+2=S (2) | 5+4=I (3) | | |
| | 4+1=E (4) | 1+0=A (1) | 16+2=R (2) | | 8+4=L (3) | | |
| 4+4=H (4) | | 10+5=O (2) | 6+7=M (1) | 6+6=L (3) | | | |
| | 2+1=C (4) | 10+3=M (2) | 1+0=A (1) | | 1+0=A (3) | | |
| | 15+6=U (2) | 17+4=U (4) | | 3+1=D (1) | | 3+0=C (3) | |
| | | 14+4=R (2) | 12+3=O (4) | 2+1=C (4) | | | |

| | | | | | | |
|---|---|---|---|---|---|---|
| 15+4=S (4) | | 5+2=G (3) | | | 2+1=C (1) | |
| | 4+1=E (4) | 10+8=R (3) | 3+1=D (3) | 1+0=A (1) | | |
| | 11+4=O (3) | 5+2=G (4) | 7+7=N (3) | 10+4=N (1) | | |
| | 10+9=S (1) | 15+6=U (3) | 1+0=A (4) | 2+2=D (1) | | 8+4=L (2) |
| | 17+2=S (2) | 4+1=E (1) | 7+5=L (1) | 6+7=M (4) | 5+4=I (2) | |
| | | 10+10=T (2) | 4+4=H (2) | 5+2=G (2) | 7+2=I (4) | |

| | | | | | | |
|---|---|---|---|---|---|---|
| | | 18+2=T (2) | 7+1=H (2) | 4+3=G (2) | 3+2=E (4) | |
| 17+2=S (1) | | | 7+2=I (2) | 14+4=R (4) | | 5+2=G (4) |
| | 14+4=R (1) | 8+4=L (2) | 2+2=D (1) | 1+0=A (1) | | 12+2=N (4) |
| | | 3+2=E (1) | 5+3=H (2) | 4+1=E (1) | 17+4=U (4) | |
| | | 5+2=G (2) | 10+3=M (3) | | 10+2=L (1) | 8+7=O (4) |
| | | 12+3=O (3) | 5+4=I (2) | 4+1=E (3) | 12+2=N (3) | 21+4=Y (4) |
| | 15+8=W (3) | | | 5+3=H (2) | | |

| | | | | | | |
|---|---|---|---|---|---|---|
| | | | 3+1=D (3) | 12+2=N (4) | | |
| | 5+2=G (1) | 3+2=E (3) | 4+1=E (4) | | 10+4=N (4) | |
| 8+6=N (1) | 16+3=S (4) | 16+2=R (4) | 14+2=P (3) | 16+3=S (2) | 5+4=I (4) | |
| | 5+4=I (1) | 5+6=K (1) | 9+7=P (3) | 2+2=D (2) | | 15+8=W (4) |
| | | 10+5=O (1) | 7+2=I (2) | 1+0=A (3) | 15+3=R (3) | 21+2=W (3) |
| | 15+3=R (2) | 1+0=A (2) | 9+6=O (1) | 11+1=L (1) | | |
| | 1+1=B (2) | | | | | |

| | | | | | | |
|---|---|---|---|---|---|---|
| | | 9+7=P (4) | 4+4=H (2) | | | |
| | | 1+0=A (2) | 9+6=O (4) | 2+1=C (2) | 3+1=D (3) | 16+2=R (4) |
| 2+1=C (1) | 1+0=A (1) | 17+2=S (2) | 15+4=S (4) | 16+2=R (2) | 3+2=E (4) | 16+2=R (3) |
| 4+1=E (1) | | 6+6=L (1) | 4+1=E (2) | 10+10=T (4) | 14+7=U (2) | 1+0=A (3) |
| | | 13+3=P (1) | | | 11+5=P (2) | 8+7=O (3) |
| | | | 3+2=E (1) | 10+6=P (3) | 1+1=B (3) | |
| | 2+1=C (3) | 7+5=L (3) | 5+4=I (3) | 14+4=R (1) | | |

| | | | | | | | |
|---|---|---|---|---|---|---|---|
| | | | 10+10=T (2) | | | | |
| | | 5+4=I (2) | 10+8=R (4) | 15+10=Y (2) | 3+2=E (3) | | |
| | | 14+4=R (2) | 12+3=O (4) | 8+4=L (3) | 14+7=U (4) | | |
| | 1+1=B (2) | 12+3=O (1) | 6+3=I (4) | 7+7=N (4) | 4+3=G (3) | 7+3=J (4) | |
| | 12+12=X (1) | 3+2=E (2) | 1+1=B (1) | | 12+2=N (3) | | |
| | 3+2=E (1) | | 6+6=L (2) | 4+1=E (2) | 2+1=C (2) | 1+0=A (3) | |
| 10+9=S (1) | | | | 17+2=S (3) | 8+8=P (3) | | |

| | | | | | | | |
|---|---|---|---|---|---|---|---|
| | | 1+0=A (4) | | | | | 10+2=L (1) |
| | | | 15+3=R (4) | | 1+0=A (1) | | |
| | 12+6=R (1) | | 10+8=R (4) | 2+1=C (1) | | | |
| 12+4=P (1) | 17+2=S (2) | 1+0=A (1) | 8+7=O (4) | 7+2=I (1) | | | |
| | 3+2=E (2) | 2+1=C (1) | 12+8=T (1) | 21+2=W (4) | 13+6=S (4) | 5+2=G (3) | |
| | 5+4=I (2) | 17+4=U (3) | 6+7=M (2) | 14+1=O (2) | 8+6=N (3) | | |
| | 2+2=D (3) | 10+3=M (2) | 16+2=R (3) | 7+2=I (3) | 8+5=M (2) | | |

## PAGE 57

| | | | | | | |
|---|---|---|---|---|---|---|
| | | | | | | |
| 2+2=D (2) | | | 15+6=U (1) | 15+3=R (1) | | |
| 4+1=E (2) | 15+5=T (4) | 12+8=T (1) | 17+4=U (4) | | 3+2=E (1) | |
| | 5+4=I (2) | 1+0=A (4) | 15+9=X (1) | 5+2=G (4) | 16+3=S (1) | |
| | | 2+0=B (2) | 6+3=I (1) | | 4+4=H (4) | |
| | 11+2=M (1) | 1+1=B (2) | 10+5=O (2) | 5+4=I (3) | 10+10=T (4) | |
| | 11+7=R (3) | 1+0=A (3) | 1+1=B (3) | 1+1=B (3) | 6+6=L (2) | |

## PAGE 58

| | | | | | | |
|---|---|---|---|---|---|---|
| | 1+0=A (1) | | | | | |
| 4+4=H (1) | 1+0=A (2) | 16+2=R (1) | 4+3=G (1) | | 12+2=N (3) | |
| 14+6=T (2) | 2+1=C (1) | | | 3+2=E (1) | 7+4=K (4) | 16+2=R (3) |
| | 11+4=O (2) | | 14+4=R (1) | | 2+1=C (4) | 3+2=E (3) |
| | | 5+6=K (2) | | | 4+4=H (3) | 6+3=I (4) |
| | 9+5=N (3) | 1+0=A (2) | 15+3=R (3) | 13+7=T (3) | 10+2=L (4) | |
| | | 8+7=O (3) | 3+1=D (2) | | | 2+1=C (4) |

| | | | | | | |
|---|---|---|---|---|---|---|
| 2+0=B (1) | | 17+2=S (3) | | 5+2=G (1) | | |
| | 3+2=E (1) | | 3+2=E (3) | 10+4=N (1) | | |
| | 2+2=D (1) | 5+2=G (2) | 5+4=I (1) | 9+3=L (3) | 17+2=S (4) | |
| | 15+4=S (2) | 3+1=D (1) | 8+6=N (2) | 2+2=D (4) | 8+1=I (3) | 11+2=M (3) |
| | | | 7+2=I (2) | 12+2=N (4) | | |
| | 5+2=G (4) | 10+8=R (4) | 1+0=A (4) | 7+4=K (2) | | |

| | | | | | | |
|---|---|---|---|---|---|---|
| | | | | 11+8=S (3) | 10+9=S (4) | |
| | | | 12+3=O (4) | 20+3=W (4) | 2+1=C (3) | |
| | | 3+1=D (4) | | | 4+4=H (3) | | 8+6=N (2) |
| | | 9+5=N (4) | 4+1=E (1) | | 12+3=O (3) | 1+0=A (2) | |
| 3+3=F (1) | 14+4=R (1) | 7+2=I (4) | 10+4=N (1) | 10+5=O (3) | 10+3=M (2) | |
| | | 21+2=W (4) | 6+6=L (3) | 2+1=C (1) | 5+4=I (2) | |
| | | | | 5+3=H (1) | 5+2=G (2) | 13+1=N (2) |

**PAGE 61**

| | | | | | | | |
|---|---|---|---|---|---|---|---|
| | | | 14+5=S (2) | 4+1=E (1) | | | |
| | | 10+9=S (2) | 5+3=H (1) | | 2+2=D (1) | | |
| | 3+2=E (2) | | 2+1=C (1) | 4+4=H (3) | | | |
| 14+4=R (2) | | 4+3=G (4) | 10+4=N (1) | | 5+2=G (3) | | |
| | 8+8=P (2) | | 12+2=N (4) | 6+3=I (1) | 15+6=U (3) | | |
| | | 13+11=X (2) | 6+3=I (4) | | 10+6=P (1) | 1+0=A (3) | |
| | 8+1=I (4) | 2+1=C (4) | 4+1=E (2) | | | 10+2=L (3) | |

**PAGE 62**

| | | | | | | |
|---|---|---|---|---|---|---|
| | 5+2=G (4) | 13+1=N (4) | | | | 4+3=G (4) |
| | 11+1=L (1) | | 5+4=I (4) | 5+1=F (4) | 5+4=I (4) | |
| 3+3=F (1) | | 4+1=E (1) | 12+8=T (4) | | 7+5=L (3) | |
| | | 17+2=S (1) | 4+1=E (3) | 12+10=V (3) | 3+2=E (3) | |
| | 13+5=R (1) | 11+8=S (3) | | 16+9=Y (1) | 1+0=A (3) | |
| | 13+6=S (2) | 14+7=U (1) | 8+7=O (1) | 2+2=D (2) | 12+3=O (2) | 1+1=B (2) |
| | | 3+2=E (2) | 6+3=I (2) | | | |

| | | | | | | |
|---|---|---|---|---|---|---|
| | 1+0=A (2) | | | | | |
| 17+4=U (2) | | | | | 11+3=N (4) | |
| 8+6=N (2) | | | 3+2=E (1) | 8+7=O (4) | | 15+3=R (3) |
| | 14+6=T (2) | 10+2=L (1) | 15+4=S (4) | 6+3=I (4) | 4+1=E (3) | |
| | 5+4=I (2) | 4+1=E (3) | 2+1=C (1) | 4+1=E (4) | 6+6=L (3) | |
| | 15+7=V (3) | 3+2=E (2) | 7+7=N (1) | 1+0=A (3) | 18+1=S (4) | |
| | 17+2=S (2) | 5+4=I (3) | 12+8=T (3) | 15+6=U (1) | | |

| | | | | | | |
|---|---|---|---|---|---|---|
| | | | | | | |
| | | | 12+4=P (1) | | | |
| | | 17+2=S (2) | 6+3=I (1) | 8+6=N (4) | 10+1=K (3) | |
| | 6+6=L (2) | 2+1=C (1) | 21+2=W (4) | 2+1=C (3) | | |
| 1+0=A (2) | | 9+6=O (4) | 5+6=K (1) | 1+0=A (3) | 4+1=E (1) | |
| | 15+7=V (2) | 10+8=R (4) | | 7+5=L (1) | 16+2=R (3) | |
| | | 13+2=O (2) | 5+2=G (4) | | | 16+4=T (3) |

| | | | | | | |
|---|---|---|---|---|---|---|
| | | | | | | |
| 5+5=J (2) | | | | | | |
| | 15+0=O (2) | | | 1+0=A (3) | | 16+3=S (4) |
| | | 6+3=I (2) | 10+10=T (3) | 7+4=K (1) | 3+2=E (3) | 4+1=E (4) |
| | 12+2=N (2) | 13+1=N (2) | 12+2=N (1) | | 11+7=R (3) | 12+2=N (4) |
| | 7+2=I (2) | 10+5=O (1) | 5+2=G (2) | | 9+6=O (4) | 17+3=T (3) |
| | | 14+5=S (1) | 12+8=T (1) | 13+13=Z (4) | | |

| | | | | | | |
|---|---|---|---|---|---|---|
| | 10+4=N (4) | 8+8=P (3) | 17+2=S (3) | | | |
| 12+3=O (4) | | | 8+1=I (3) | 21+4=Y (1) | | 1+0=A (2) |
| | 6+3=I (4) | 15+6=U (2) | 7+7=N (3) | | 6+6=L (1) | 7+5=L (2) |
| | 15+5=T (4) | 11+7=R (3) | 6+7=M (2) | | 6+3=I (1) | 10+2=L (2) |
| | 1+0=A (4) | 18+3=U (3) | 1+1=B (2) | 11+2=M (1) | 3+2=E (2) | |
| | 13+7=T (3) | 2+1=C (4) | 1+0=A (1) | 15+3=R (2) | | |
| | 1+0=A (4) | 17+5=V (4) | | 5+1=F (1) | | |

**PAGE 67**

| | | | | | | |
|---|---|---|---|---|---|---|
| | 16+3=S (4) | 8+6=N (4) | 10+8=R (4) | 4+1=E (4) | | |
| | | 2+1=C (4) | 3+2=E (4) | 16+2=R (3) | | |
| | 6+6=L (1) | | 14+12=Z (1) | 4+1=E (3) | | |
| 3+2=E (2) | 17+2=S (2) | 5+4=I (1) | 10+2=L (3) | 1+0=A (1) | | |
| | 13+11=X (2) | | 1+0=A (3) | | 15+3=R (1) | |
| | | 1+0=A (2) | | 3+2=E (3) | | 1+1=B (1) |
| | | | 20+3=W (2) | | 2+2=D (3) | |

**PAGE 68**

| | | | | | | |
|---|---|---|---|---|---|---|
| | 2+1=C (4) | 6+3=I (4) | | 17+2=S (4) | | 7+3=J (4) |
| 4+1=E (4) | | 14+5=S (2) | 10+10=T (4) | 17+2=S (2) | 16+5=U (4) | |
| | 14+4=R (2) | | | 5+4=I (2) | | |
| | 4+3=G (1) | 3+2=E (2) | 12+2=N (2) | | | |
| | | 11+4=O (1) | 6+1=G (2) | | 10+2=L (1) | |
| | | 16+3=S (1) | 11+3=N (3) | 3+2=E (1) | | |
| | | 5+6=K (3) | 8+8=P (1) | 14+7=U (3) | 15+3=R (3) | 2+2=D (3) |

**PAGE 69**

| | | | | | | |
|---|---|---|---|---|---|---|
| | | 3+2=E (1) | | | | |
| | 11+7=R (1) | 14+6=T (2) | 2+2=D (1) | | | 5+2=G (3) |
| | 17+2=S (2) | 4+1=E (1) | 12+2=N (2) | 7+2=I (2) | 10+4=N (3) | |
| | | 4+4=H (1) | 16+2=R (3) | 4+5=I (3) | 12+3=O (2) | 6+4=J (2) |
| | | 1+0=A (3) | 12+8=T (1) | 12+7=S (4) | | |
| | 7+1=H (3) | 4+1=E (4) | 10+2=L (4) | 10+5=O (1) | 6+3=I (4) | |
| 11+8=S (3) | | 16+3=S (4) | | 1+1=B (1) | | 1+0=A (4) |

**PAGE 70**

| | | | | | | |
|---|---|---|---|---|---|---|
| | | | | 18+1=S (3) | | |
| | | | 14+4=R (3) | 4+1=E (2) | | |
| | 12+3=O (1) | 2+2=D (1) | 10+10=T (2) | 3+2=E (3) | 15+3=R (2) | |
| | 8+7=O (1) | 1+0=A (2) | 7+5=L (1) | 10+10=T (3) | | |
| 10+4=N (1) | 3+2=E (2) | 12+8=T (4) | 3+2=E (1) | | 12+8=T (3) | |
| | 1+0=A (4) | 17+6=W (2) | 19+1=T (4) | 17+2=S (1) | 1+0=A (3) | |
| 2+1=C (4) | | 16+3=S (2) | | 8+4=L (4) | 3+2=E (4) | 6+7=M (3) |

**PAGE 71**

| | | | | | | |
|---|---|---|---|---|---|---|
| | 16+2=R (4) | | 17+2=S (3) | 4+1=E (4) | | |
| | 3+1=D (4) | 1+0=A (4) | 12+2=N (4) | 3+1=D (3) | 8+5=M (4) | |
| 16+3=S (4) | | 17+1=R (2) | | 8+6=N (3) | | 17+2=S (3) |
| | | 4+1=E (2) | 2+1=C (1) | 5+3=H (1) | 14+1=O (3) | 4+1=E (3) |
| | 1+1=B (2) | 15+3=R (1) | | | 2+1=C (3) | |
| | 6+7=M (2) | 1+0=A (1) | 3+0=C (2) | 4+1=E (2) | 2+2=D (2) | |
| | | 3+2=E (2) | 11+2=M (1) | | | |

**PAGE 72**

| | | | | | | |
|---|---|---|---|---|---|---|
| | 10+4=N (4) | 9+6=O (1) | | | | |
| | 5+4=I (1) | 4+1=E (4) | 8+6=N (1) | | | 14+11=Y (2) |
| | 10+2=L (4) | 12+8=T (1) | 15+3=R (2) | | 2+1=C (2) | 18+7=Y (3) |
| 7+5=L (4) | | 17+4=U (2) | 14+5=S (1) | 1+0=A (2) | 6+6=L (3) | |
| | 12+3=O (4) | 3+0=C (2) | | 4+1=E (1) | 19+2=U (3) | |
| | 2+1=C (2) | 21+2=W (4) | | 14+7=U (1) | 13+5=R (3) | |
| | 16+3=S (4) | 1+0=A (2) | | 10+10=T (3) | 11+6=Q (1) | |

| | | | | | | |
|---|---|---|---|---|---|---|
| 5+2=G (3) | | | 3+2=E (1) | | | |
| | 12+2=N (3) | 8+6=N (1) | 15+4=S (2) | 10+1=K (1) | | |
| | 5+4=I (3) | 1+0=A (2) | 2+1=C (1) | 10+10=T (2) | | |
| | 4+1=E (2) | 9+2=K (3) | 2+2=D (4) | 7+2=I (1) | | |
| | 16+2=R (2) | 5+4=I (4) | 1+0=A (3) | 1+0=A (4) | 5+3=H (1) | |
| | 7+7=N (4) | 2+0=B (2) | 4+4=H (3) | 4+1=E (4) | | 2+1=C (1) |
| | 4+3=G (4) | 18+1=S (4) | | 17+2=S (3) | 6+2=H (4) | |

| | | | | | | |
|---|---|---|---|---|---|---|
| | | | | | | 2+1=C (4) |
| 10+2=L (2) | 1+0=A (2) | | | | | 19+2=U (4) |
| | | 15+3=R (2) | 1+0=A (1) | | 16+2=R (4) | |
| | | 12+8=T (1) | 14+7=U (2) | 1+1=B (1) | 8+4=L (4) | |
| | | 14+6=T (1) | 15+5=T (2) | 17+2=S (4) | | 15+8=W (3) |
| | 6+6=L (1) | 14+5=S (3) | 1+0=A (2) | 14+8=V (3) | 4+1=E (3) | |
| | 2+3=E (1) | | 3+2=E (3) | 8+6=N (2) | 1+0=A (3) | |

| | | | | | | |
|---|---|---|---|---|---|---|
| 4+3=G (4) | 16+2=R (2) | | | 13+6=S (1) | | |
| 16+2=R (4) | 3+2=E (2) | | 7+7=N (1) | 3+2=E (3) | 18+1=S (3) | |
| 10+10=T (2) | 4+1=E (4) | 10+4=N (4) | 9+3=L (3) | 4+5=I (1) | | |
| 10+4=N (2) | 3+2=E (4) | 2+1=C (3) | 20+2=V (4) | | 1+0=A (1) | 4+1=E (4) |
| | 4+1=E (2) | 5+4=I (3) | 7+2=I (4) | 10+8=R (1) | 7+5=L (4) | |
| | 14+6=T (3) | 2+1=C (2) | | 10+2=L (4) | 17+3=T (1) | |
| | | 16+2=R (3) | 1+0=A (3) | | | |

**PAGE 76**

| | | | | | | |
|---|---|---|---|---|---|---|
| | | 6+3=I (1) | 12+2=N (1) | | 17+1=R (3) | |
| | | 4+3=G (1) | 6+5=K (1) | 17+2=S (2) | 1+1=B (3) | 3+2=E (3) |
| | | 4+1=E (2) | 11+7=R (2) | 8+7=O (1) | 2+2=D (3) | 8+1=I (3) |
| | 5+3=H (4) | | 17+3=T (2) | 9+6=O (1) | 7+7=N (3) | 10+2=L (3) |
| | | 3+2=E (4) | 2+1=C (1) | 14+4=R (2) | 15+5=T (3) | 1+0=A (3) |
| 16+2=R (4) | 1+0=A (4) | 10+10=T (2) | 1+0=A (2) | | 11+11=V (3) | |
| | 3+1=D (4) | | 17+2=S (2) | | | |

**PAGE 77**

| | | | | | | |
|---|---|---|---|---|---|---|
| | | 4+1=E (3) | | | | |
| | | | 12+8=T (3) | 8+6=N (1) | | |
| | 3+2=E (1) | 1+0=A (1) | 7+2=I (3) | 8+7=O (1) | | |
| 21+2=W (1) | 11+7=R (4) | | 8+8=P (1) | 16+2=R (3) | | |
| | | 3+2=E (4) | | | 11+5=P (3) | 18+1=S (3) |
| | 18+2=T (2) | 18+4=V (4) | 4+1=E (2) | 1+1=B (2) | | |
| | | 8+4=L (2) | 10+2=L (4) | 4+5=I (4) | 10+9=S (4) | |

**PAGE 78**

| | | | | | | | |
|---|---|---|---|---|---|---|---|
| | | | | 10+6=P (1) | | | |
| | | | 1+0=A (1) | | 5+3=H (4) | 2+1=C (4) | |
| | | 18+1=S (2) | | 12+1=M (1) | 1+0=A (4) | | |
| | 10+9=S (1) | 16+4=T (2) | 12+7=S (4) | 11+5=P (1) | 5+4=I (4) | | |
| | 14+4=R (2) | 12+6=R (1) | 3+2=E (1) | 16+2=R (4) | | 21+1=V (3) | |
| 2+2=D (3) | 3+2=E (3) | 1+0=A (2) | 14+7=U (3) | 10+10=T (3) | 4+1=E (3) | | |
| | | 13+5=R (3) | 12+4=P (2) | 1+0=A (2) | 10+4=N (3) | | |

| | | | | | | | |
|---|---|---|---|---|---|---|---|
| | | | | | | | |
| | | | 10+9=S (1) | | | | |
| 7+1=H (3) | | 15+3=R (1) | | | | | |
| | 10+9=S (3) | 8+7=O (1) | 15+8=W (2) | 4+1=E (2) | 6+6=L (2) | | |
| 3+2=E (4) | 7+2=I (3) | | 14+4=R (1) | | | 2+0=B (2) | |
| 8+4=L (4) | 14+4=R (3) | | 11+7=R (1) | 3+2=E (1) | | | |
| 7+2=I (3) | 3+1=D (4) | 11+3=N (4) | 13+8=U (4) | 1+1=B (4) | | | |

| | | | | | | | |
|---|---|---|---|---|---|---|---|
| | 1+0=A (1) | 4+3=G (1) | | | | | |
| 7+4=K (1) | | 17+1=R (3) | 3+2=E (1) | | | | |
| | 2+1=C (1) | 15+4=S (1) | 4+1=E (3) | | 5+2=G (4) | 16+2=R (3) | |
| | 1+0=A (1) | | 2+2=D (3) | 7+7=N (4) | 3+2=E (3) | | |
| | 10+10=T (2) | 8+8=P (1) | 7+2=I (4) | 1+0=A (3) | | | |
| | 7+2=I (2) | 1+0=A (2) | 15+3=R (4) | 12+3=O (2) | 4+4=H (2) | | |
| | 10+2=L (2) | 9+7=P (2) | 15+4=S (2) | 11+7=R (4) | 1+0=A (4) | 3+2=E (4) | |

|  |  |  |  |  |  |  |
|---|---|---|---|---|---|---|
|  |  | 4+3=G (3) | 8+6=N (1) | 17+2=S (1) |  | 10+9=S (2) |
|  | 11+3=N (3) | 13+2=O (1) | 3+0=C (4) | 4+4=H (4) | 4+1=E (2) |  |
|  | 7+2=I (3) | 5+4=I (1) | 10+10=T (4) | 2+1=C (2) | 3+2=E (4) |  |
|  | 5+6=K (3) | 8+1=I (4) | 12+8=T (1) | 1+0=A (2) |  | 14+5=S (4) |
|  | 17+3=T (4) | 11+7=R (3) | 11+5=P (1) |  | 14+4=R (2) |  |
| 16+3=S (4) |  | 10+5=O (1) | 1+0=A (3) |  | 1+1=B (2) |  |
|  |  |  | 2+2=D (3) |  |  |  |

**PAGE 82**

|  |  |  |  |  |  |  |
|---|---|---|---|---|---|---|
| 3+3=F (1) |  |  | 10+10=T (2) |  |  |  |
| 8+1=I (1) |  |  | 1+0=A (2) |  | 3+2=E (2) | 16+3=S (4) |
|  | 10+9=S (1) | 6+6=L (2) |  | 10+9=S (1) | 14+4=R (4) |  |
|  | 14+2=P (2) | 5+3=H (1) | 3+2=E (1) | 12+8=T (3) | 18+7=Y (3) | 14+7=U (4) |
|  |  | 6+7=M (2) | 15+4=S (3) |  | 3+0=C (4) |  |
|  | 9+5=N (3) | 1+0=A (3) | 4+1=E (2) | 17+3=T (2) |  | 3+0=C (4) |
|  |  |  |  |  | 10+5=O (4) |  |

| | | | | | | |
|---|---|---|---|---|---|---|
| | | 13+6=S (2) | | | | 15+5=T (1) |
| | 9+3=L (2) | 3+2=E (3) | 4+1=E (3) | 7+2=I (1) | 5+3=H (1) | |
| | 10+9=S (3) | 1+0=A (2) | 11+3=N (1) | 3+2=E (4) | 10+9=S (4) | |
| 16+3=S (3) | | | 2+1=C (2) | 6+1=G (1) | 15+4=S (4) | |
| | 3+2=E (3) | | 12+3=O (2) | 16+2=R (4) | 14+5=S (1) | |
| | 8+6=N (3) | 11+1=L (2) | | | 16+5=U (4) | 9+5=N (4) |
| | | 12+2=N (3) | 4+1=E (3) | 13+7=T (3) | | |

| | | | | | | |
|---|---|---|---|---|---|---|
| | | | 6+1=G (2) | | | |
| | 4+1=E (1) | | | 12+2=N (2) | | 18+1=S (4) |
| 3+3=F (1) | 12+6=R (1) | 1+0=A (1) | 6+3=I (2) | | 4+1=E (4) | |
| | 15+4=S (1) | 15+5=T (2) | | 6+2=H (4) | 17+2=S (3) | |
| | | 1+0=A (2) | 3+2=E (2) | 4+1=E (3) | 16+3=S (4) | |
| | 10+5=O (3) | 6+6=L (3) | 21+1=V (3) | 6+2=H (2) | | 1+0=A (4) |
| | | 22+1=W (3) | | | 7+5=L (4) | |

| | | | | | | |
|---|---|---|---|---|---|---|
| 10+2=L (1) | | | 9+7=P (4) | | | |
| | 4+1=E (1) | | 14+4=R (4) | 11+11=V (3) | | |
| | 1+0=A (1) | 11+4=O (4) | | 4+1=E (3) | | |
| | 8+5=M (4) | 7+4=K (1) | 5+3=H (3) | | 2+1=C (3) | 15+4=S (2) |
| | 12+6=R (2) | 7+2=I (1) | | 4+5=I (3) | 6+7=M (2) | 11+1=L (3) |
| | | 4+1=E (2) | 8+6=N (1) | 4+3=G (1) | 1+0=A (2) | 4+1=E (3) |
| | | | 8+4=L (2) | 10+2=L (2) | | |

| | | | | | | |
|---|---|---|---|---|---|---|
| | 1+1=B (4) | | | 7+2=I (3) | | |
| 14+1=O (4) | | 11+5=P (2) | | | 20+6=Z (3) | |
| 12+8=T (4) | 1+0=A (2) | | | 15+4=S (1) | 12+6=R (2) | 13+13=Z (3) |
| 18+2=T (4) | 2+1=C (2) | 11+2=M (4) | 7+8=O (1) | 3+2=E (2) | 5+2=G (1) | 14+7=U (3) |
| | 8+7=O (4) | 7+2=I (2) | 10+3=M (1) | 5+4=I (2) | 7+7=N (1) | 2+1=C (3) |
| | | 4+1=E (1) | 4+2=F (2) | 7+2=I (1) | 1+0=A (3) | |
| | | 10+10=T (1) | 4+4=H (1) | | | 8+2=J (3) |

**PAGE 87**

| | | | | | | |
|---|---|---|---|---|---|---|
| | | | 13+6=S (4) | | | |
| | | | | 2+1=C (4) | | |
| | | 4+1=E (1) | 5+0=E (4) | 4+1=E (4) | 12+7=S (3) | |
| | 2+1=C (1) | 10+10=T (2) | 14+4=R (1) | 10+4=N (4) | 6+5=K (3) | |
| | 3+2=E (2) | 10+9=S (2) | | 3+2=E (1) | 12+2=N (3) | 5+4=I (3) |
| | 15+3=R (2) | 8+1=I (2) | | 1+0=A (1) | 13+1=N (3) | |
| 11+8=S (2) | | 17+2=S (2) | | 21+4=Y (3) | 11+1=L (1) | |

**PAGE 88**

| | | | | | | |
|---|---|---|---|---|---|---|
| 15+3=R (4) | 3+2=E (4) | | | | | 4+3=G (3) |
| 11+10=U (4) | 16+3=S (1) | 11+8=S (4) | 5+2=G (2) | | 8+6=N (3) | |
| | 10+10=T (4) | 3+1=D (1) | | 10+4=N (2) | 5+1=F (1) | 7+2=I (3) |
| 2+1=C (4) | | 12+2=N (1) | 5+4=I (2) | | 10+8=R (1) | 6+1=G (3) |
| 6+3=I (4) | | 10+1=K (2) | 3+2=E (1) | 5+4=I (1) | | 12+2=N (3) |
| 9+7=P (4) | | 16+3=S (2) | | | 6+3=I (3) | |
| | | | 1+0=A (2) | | 11+7=R (3) | |

|  |  |  |  |  |  |  |
|---|---|---|---|---|---|---|
|  |  |  |  | 11+2=M (2) |  |  |
| 4+3=G (3) |  | 14+5=S (2) | 11+5=P (2) |  | 7+2=I (2) |  |
|  | 8+6=N (3) |  | 2+1=C (1) |  | 4+4=H (2) |  |
|  |  | 8+1=I (3) |  | 1+0=A (1) |  | 17+6=W (2) |
|  |  |  | 21+2=W (3) | 8+5=M (1) |  |  |
|  | 1+0=A (1) | 15+3=R (4) | 4+1=E (1) | 11+4=O (3) | 10+4=N (3) | 18+1=S (4) |
|  | 4+2=F (4) | 10+8=R (1) | 8+7=O (4) | 7+7=N (4) | 12+8=T (4) | 9+2=K (3) |

|  |  |  |  |  |  |  |
|---|---|---|---|---|---|---|
| 15+5=T (3) |  |  |  |  |  | 11+12=W (2) |
|  | 4+4=H (3) |  |  |  | 4+1=E (2) |  |
|  | 15+3=R (3) | 10+9=S (1) |  |  | 2+3=E (2) |  |
|  | 5+4=I (3) | 12+2=N (1) | 12+7=S (2) | 2+2=D (2) |  |  |
|  |  | 10+2=L (3) | 7+2=I (1) | 9+5=N (4) | 4+1=E (4) |  |
|  |  | 7+5=L (3) | 13+7=T (4) | 15+8=W (1) |  | 18+2=T (4) |
|  |  | 6+2=H (4) |  | 13+7=T (1) |  |  |

| | | | | | | |
|---|---|---|---|---|---|---|
| | 11+8=S (4) | | | | 16+2=R (3) | |
| | | 1+0=A (4) | 10+4=N (4) | 2+2=D (4) | 1+0=A (3) | |
| | 14+5=S (1) | 3+2=E (1) | 11+1=L (1) | | 19+4=W (4) | 10+1=K (3) |
| | | 16+4=T (1) | 8+4=L (2) | 10+2=L (1) | 3+2=E (3) | 5+4=I (4) |
| | 15+3=R (2) | 8+7=O (2) | 7+5=L (2) | 1+0=A (1) | 2+1=C (4) | 16+3=S (3) |
| | 12+8=T (2) | | | 3+2=E (2) | 14+6=T (1) | 6+2=H (4) |
| 18+1=S (2) | | | | | 13+5=R (2) | |

| | | | | | | |
|---|---|---|---|---|---|---|
| | 10+9=S (4) | | | | 6+1=G (4) | 11+3=N (4) |
| | | 6+3=I (4) | | 11+5=P (2) | 9+0=I (4) | |
| | 4+2=F (1) | | 2+0=B (4) | 10+2=L (4) | 14+4=R (2) | |
| | | 10+2=L (1) | 2+1=C (2) | 7+2=I (2) | | |
| | 1+0=A (3) | 5+4=I (1) | | 9+2=K (2) | 4+3=G (1) | |
| 3+1=D (3) | 12+6=R (1) | 15+4=S (3) | 1+0=A (3) | 12+2=N (1) | | |
| | | 12+8=T (1) | 6+3=I (1) | 7+7=N (3) | 8+1=I (3) | |

| | | | | | | |
|---|---|---|---|---|---|---|
| | | | | | | |
| | | | | 11+8=S (1) | 15+4=S (1) | 17+2=S (3) |
| | 15+10=Y (2) | | 4+1=E (1) | | 3+2=E (1) | 3+1=D (3) |
| 10+5=O (2) | 9+7=P (4) | 10+2=L (1) | | | 12+6=R (3) | 17+2=S (1) |
| | 2+0=B (2) | 1+0=A (4) | 1+1=B (1) | 3+2=E (3) | | |
| | 14+9=W (2) | | 3+0=C (4) | | 4+4=H (3) | |
| | | 11+4=O (2) | 2+1=C (2) | 4+1=E (4) | 14+4=R (4) | |

| | | | | | | |
|---|---|---|---|---|---|---|
| | | | 11+8=S (2) | 9+6=O (4) | 14+6=T (4) | |
| | | 19+2=U (2) | 16+2=R (4) | 18+1=S (4) | | |
| | | 14+4=R (4) | 8+8=P (2) | | 8+7=O (2) | |
| | 14+7=U (1) | 1+0=A (4) | 14+1=O (2) | | 2+1=C (2) | 3+1=D (3) |
| 1+0=A (1) | 2+1=C (4) | 4+3=G (1) | 1+0=A (3) | 12+8=T (2) | | 3+2=E (3) |
| | 5+2=G (3) | 12+6=R (3) | 20+1=U (1) | 12+2=N (3) | 15+5=T (3) | |
| | | | 16+3=S (1) | 10+10=T (1) | | |

| | | | | | | |
|---|---|---|---|---|---|---|
| | | | | | 20+1=U (4) | 1+1=B (4) |
| | | 11+5=P (2) | | 6+7=M (4) | | |
| | | | 15+3=R (2) | 14+2=P (4) | 17+2=S (4) | |
| | 4+2=F (2) | | 13+2=O (2) | 6+7=M (1) | 10+6=P (3) | |
| 4+1=E (3) | | 11+4=O (2) | 6+1=G (1) | 4+3=G (3) | 1+0=A (1) | 15+6=U (3) |
| | 2+2=D (3) | 11+3=N (1) | 12+6=R (3) | 6+3=I (1) | | |
| | | 1+0=A (3) | 5+4=I (1) | 11+1=L (1) | | |

| | | | | | | |
|---|---|---|---|---|---|---|
| | | | | | | |
| | | 4+1=E (1) | 11+1=L (3) | 2+0=B (3) | | |
| | 3+0=C (1) | 15+4=S (4) | 12+6=R (4) | 3+2=E (3) | 1+1=B (3) | 6+7=M (2) |
| | 12+2=N (1) | 11+4=O (4) | 1+0=A (1) | 19+2=U (2) | 12+3=O (2) | 4+5=I (3) |
| | 10+3=M (4) | 1+0=A (1) | 10+10=T (2) | 15+3=R (1) | | 16+2=I (3) |
| 1+0=A (4) | 11+7=R (4) | 4+3=G (1) | 5+3=H (2) | 11+7=R (1) | | 3+1=D (3) |
| | | | 8+7=O (1) | | | |

| | | | | | | |
|---|---|---|---|---|---|---|
| | | 5+4=I (1) | | | | 1+0=A (4) |
| | 10+5=O (1) | | 12+8=T (1) | | 6+6=L (4) | |
| 4+1=E (2) | 10+8=R (2) | 7+7=N (1) | 4+1=E (3) | 1+0=A (1) | 10+10=T (4) | |
| | 5+6=K (2) | 17+2=S (1) | 7+2=I (3) | 14+4=R (1) | | 3+2=E (4) |
| | | 2+1=C (2) | 5+2=G (3) | 8+8=P (1) | 3+2=E (1) | 15+3=R (4) |
| | | 9+6=O (2) | 12+3=O (1) | 4+3=G (3) | | 18+1=S (4) |
| | 11+7=R (2) | | | 3+2=E (3) | 15+7=V (3) | |

| | | | | | | |
|---|---|---|---|---|---|---|
| 11+7=R (2) | | | | | 17+2=S (1) | |
| | 4+1=E (2) | | | 11+7=R (1) | | |
| | | 8+6=N (2) | 13+1=N (4) | | 7+2=I (1) | 3+1=D (4) |
| | 1+1=B (4) | 1+0=A (4) | 7+7=N (2) | 2+2=D (4) | 11+4=O (1) | 7+2=I (4) |
| | | | 1+0=A (2) | 4+4=H (1) | 1+0=A (4) | |
| | 13+2=O (3) | | 2+1=C (1) | 10+2=L (2) | 9+7=P (2) | |
| | | 10+3=M (3) | 5+4=I (3) | 10+10=T (3) | 14+5=S (3) | |

| | | | | | | |
|---|---|---|---|---|---|---|
| | 12+13=Y (3) | 1+0=A (3) | | | | |
| | | 3+1=D (3) | 8+8=P (1) | 11+2=M (1) | | |
| | 21+4=Y (2) | 9+6=O (1) | 4+4=H (3) | 11+4=O (1) | | |
| | 6+6=L (2) | 18+1=S (1) | 12+8=T (3) | | 2+1=C (1) | |
| | 3+2=E (1) | 5+6=K (2) | | 14+4=R (3) | 6+3=I (3) | |
| | 4+1=E (4) | 3+2=E (2) | 4+1=E (2) | 21+2=W (2) | | 1+1=B (3) |
| 16+2=R (4) | 17+2=S (4) | 12+1=M (4) | 15+3=R (4) | 1+0=A (4) | 5+1=F (4) | |

| | | | | | | |
|---|---|---|---|---|---|---|
| | | | | | | |
| | 4+1=E (2) | 10+10=T (1) | 17+2=S (1) | | | |
| 15+10=Y (2) | 3+2=E (1) | 14+4=R (2) | 12+3=O (1) | | | |
| 3+1=D (1) | 15+8=W (2) | 3+1=D (4) | 17+2=S (2) | 10+8=R (1) | 3+3=F (1) | 18+1=S (4) |
| | 16+3=S (3) | 1+0=A (2) | 8+7=O (4) | 7+7=N (4) | 2+1=C (3) | 16+4=T (4) |
| | 7+5=L (2) | 14+6=T (3) | 5+4=I (3) | 8+4=L (3) | 14+7=U (4) | |
| | | 3+2=E (3) | 8+6=N (3) | | | |

| | | | | | | |
|---|---|---|---|---|---|---|
| | 2+1=C (2) | | 3+0=C (1) | 5+3=H (1) | | 16+2=R (2) |
| | 17+4=U (2) | 14+4=R (1) | | 3+2=E (3) | 4+1=E (2) | 11+8=S (4) |
| 8+8=P (1) | 10+5=O (1) | 2+1=C (2) | 6+6=L (3) | | 1+1=B (2) | 3+2=E (4) |
| | | 3+1=D (3) | 10+11=U (2) | 6+7=M (2) | | 15+4=S (4) |
| | | 2+2=D (3) | | | 6+3=I (4) | |
| | | | 7+2=I (3) | 13+5=R (3) | 18+3=U (4) | |
| | | | | 17+1=R (4) | 1+1=B (4) | |

| | | | | | | |
|---|---|---|---|---|---|---|
| | | 12+7=S (4) | | | | |
| | | 11+2=M (4) | 21+4=Y (4) | | 15+3=R (3) | |
| | 3+2=E (4) | 15+4=S (1) | 11+8=S (4) | 4+1=E (3) | | |
| 17+2=S (1) | | 10+10=T (4) | 14+6=T (1) | | 11+2=M (3) | 14+1=O (3) |
| | 4+1=E (1) | 11+8=S (2) | 1+0=A (1) | | 7+5=L (2) | 16+2=R (3) |
| | 11+1=L (1) | 8+8=P (1) | 7+5=L (2) | 1+0=A (2) | 18+1=S (3) | |
| | | 4+1=E (2) | 1+1=B (2) | | | 3+2=E (3) |

| | | | | | | | |
|---|---|---|---|---|---|---|---|
| | | | | | | | |
| 2+1=C (3) | | | | | | | |
| | 14+7=U (3) | | 18+1=S (4) | 4+3=G (1) | 14+5=S (1) | | |
| | 15+3=R (3) | 3+2=E (3) | 1+0=A (1) | 6+6=L (4) | 5+4=I (4) | | |
| | | 17+2=S (3) | 10+2=L (1) | 1+0=A (4) | | 3+2=E (2) | |
| | | 4+1=E (2) | 12+8=T (4) | 3+3=F (1) | 3+0=C (2) | | |
| | 10+4=N (2) | 5+3=H (2) | 1+0=A (2) | 7+7=N (2) | | | |

**PAGE 104**

| | | | | | | | |
|---|---|---|---|---|---|---|---|
| | | 4+3=G (2) | 8+6=N (3) | | | | |
| | 11+3=N (2) | 8+7=O (3) | 12+6=R (1) | 3+2=E (1) | | | |
| | | 4+5=I (2) | 7+2=I (3) | 2+2=D (4) | 6+3=I (1) | | |
| | | 14+8=V (2) | 14+4=R (4) | 9+7=P (3) | 11+8=S (1) | | |
| | 13+2=O (2) | 8+1=I (4) | 6+7=M (3) | | 1+0=A (1) | | |
| | 4+4=H (4) | 11+2=M (2) | 1+0=A (3) | | | 4+1=E (1) | |
| 10+10=T (4) | | | | 5+3=H (3) | 2+1=C (3) | | |

**PAGE 105**

| | | | | | | |
|---|---|---|---|---|---|---|
| | | | | | | |
| | | | 16+2=R (2) | 18+1=S (2) | | 4+1=E (4) |
| | 11+8=S (1) | 12+3=O (2) | 1+0=A (1) | 6+2=H (3) | 6+6=L (4) | |
| | 11+4=O (2) | 15+5=T (1) | 2+1=C (3) | 4+1=E (1) | | 3+1=D (4) |
| 10+2=L (2) | | 11+3=N (3) | | 6+2=H (1) | 2+2=D (4) | |
| 5+1=F (2) | 15+6=U (3) | | | 1+0=A (4) | 2+1=C (1) | |
| | 15+3=R (3) | 3+0=C (3) | | 10+9=S (4) | | |

**PAGE 106**

| | | | | | | |
|---|---|---|---|---|---|---|
| | 12+7=S (3) | | | 5+3=H (3) | | |
| | | 13+2=O (3) | 15+5=T (3) | | 4+1=E (3) | |
| | | 17+4=U (3) | 15+3=R (2) | | | 13+5=R (3) |
| | | 5+6=K (1) | 1+0=A (2) | | 10+10=T (1) | 7+7=N (3) |
| | 7+5=L (1) | 10+2=L (2) | 2+1=C (1) | 1+0=A (1) | | |
| 4+3=G (4) | 4+1=E (1) | | 8+7=O (2) | 2+2=D (4) | 3+2=E (4) | |
| | 12+2=N (4) | 5+4=I (4) | 3+1=D (4) | 9+7=P (2) | | 14+9=W (4) |

**PAGE 107**

| | | | | | | |
|---|---|---|---|---|---|---|
| | | | | | | |
| | | 21+2=W (3) | | 8+6=N (3) | | |
| | 1+1=B (3) | | 4+1=E (3) | | 3+2=E (2) | |
| | 11+3=N (1) | 11+4=O (3) | | | 10+2=L (2) | 4+1=E (4) |
| 10+5=O (1) | | 6+3=I (1) | 14+4=R (3) | 2+2=D (2) | 21+4=Y (4) | 17+1=R (4) |
| | | 9+5=N (3) | 9+6=O (1) | 15+3=R (4) | 4+1=E (2) | 11+8=S (2) |
| | | | 12+2=N (1) | 14+5=S (1) | 2+2=D (4) | 10+8=R (2) |

**PAGE 108**

| | | | | | | |
|---|---|---|---|---|---|---|
| | 2+1=C (3) | | | 4+1=E (4) | | |
| | 1+0=A (3) | 16+2=R (2) | | 10+2=L (4) | 15+5=T (4) | 10+10=T (1) |
| | 8+7=O (2) | 17+1=R (3) | 4+1=E (4) | | 6+6=L (1) | |
| | 14+7=U (2) | 2+1=C (4) | 11+7=R (3) | | | 17+4=U (1) |
| | 1+0=A (4) | 12+8=T (2) | 2+2=D (1) | 8+1=I (3) | 2+1=C (1) | 18+1=S (3) |
| 10+8=R (4) | | 5+4=I (1) | 4+1=E (2) | 1+0=A (3) | 7+2=I (1) | 4+1=E (3) |
| | 2+0=B (4) | | 4+2=F (1) | 5+1=F (1) | 5+2=G (3) | |

**PAGE 109**

| | | | | | | |
|---|---|---|---|---|---|---|
| 5+1=F (1) | | | 5+2=G (2) | | | |
| | 1+0=A (1) | 7+7=N (2) | | | 10+10=T (4) | |
| | 2+1=C (1) | 5+4=I (2) | 1+0=A (1) | 5+7=L (1) | | 18+1=S (4) |
| | 15+8=W (2) | 5+4=I (1) | | 3+1=D (3) | 7+2=I (3) | 3+2=E (4) |
| | | 9+6=O (2) | 2+2=D (3) | | 4+3=G (4) | 12+2=N (3) |
| | | 1+0=A (3) | 6+6=L (2) | 2+0=B (2) | 6+1=G (3) | 5+2=G (4) |
| | 10+6=P (3) | | | 15+4=S (4) | 11+10=U (4) | |

**PAGE 110**

| | | | | | | |
|---|---|---|---|---|---|---|
| | | 1+1=B (4) | | | | |
| | 3+2=E (2) | 1+0=A (4) | 12+7=S (3) | | | |
| 1+0=A (2) | 2+1=C (4) | 9+2=K (4) | 2+1=C (3) | 3+3=F (1) | | |
| 14+5=S (2) | 6+3=I (4) | 5+4=I (3) | | 4+1=E (1) | 15+3=R (3) | |
| 11+3=N (4) | 12+8=T (2) | 10+9=S (3) | 1+0=A (1) | 10+5=O (3) | | |
| 4+3=G (4) | 14+4=R (2) | 3+2=E (2) | 16+3=S (3) | 18+2=T (1) | 14+7=U (1) | |
| | | | | 11+8=S (1) | 3+2=E (1) | 15+3=R (1) |

| | | | | | | | |
|---|---|---|---|---|---|---|---|
| | | | 2+2=D (1) | | | | |
| | | 12+8=T (2) | 17+2=S (2) | 4+1=E (1) | | | |
| | 14+4=R (2) | | 10+10=T (4) | | 3+3=F (1) | | |
| | | 1+0=A (2) | 11+7=R (4) | 12+2=N (1) | 4+1=E (1) | | |
| 21+4=Y (3) | 3+2=E (3) | 16+5=U (2) | 16+3=S (1) | 5+4=I (4) | | | 17+2=S (4) |
| | 12+5=Q (2) | 10+1=K (3) | 3+2=E (1) | 14+7=U (4) | 11+6=Q (4) | | |
| | | | 12+2=N (3) | 11+4=O (3) | 7+6=M (3) | | |

| | | | | | | | |
|---|---|---|---|---|---|---|---|
| 2+1=C (4) | | | 3+2=E (1) | | | | |
| | 10+8=R (4) | 6+3=I (2) | 10+10=T (2) | 5+3=H (1) | | | |
| | 1+0=A (4) | 19+2=U (2) | 4+1=E (2) | 4+4=H (3) | 14+6=T (1) | | |
| | 15+4=S (2) | 20+6=Z (4) | 2+1=C (3) | 1+0=A (1) | | | |
| | | 15+10=Y (4) | 1+1=B (1) | 6+6=L (3) | | | |
| | | | | | | 3+2=E (3) | 17+6=W (3) |

| | | | | | | |
|---|---|---|---|---|---|---|
| | | 8+1=I (2) | 7+5=L (1) | 2+2=D (1) | | |
| | 5+3=H (2) | 5+4=I (1) | 2+1=C (2) | 16+3=S (2) | 12+2=N (1) | 4+3=G (4) |
| | 7+7=N (1) | 8+8=P (2) | | 14+5=S (3) | 1+0=A (1) | 8+6=N (4) |
| | | 4+3=G (1) | 1+0=A (2) | 4+4=H (1) | 4+1=E (3) | 8+1=I (4) |
| 3+2=E (3) | 14+4=R (3) | 14+4=R (2) | 7+2=I (3) | 2+1=C (3) | | 12+8=T (4) |
| | 11+8=S (3) | 12+10=V (3) | 5+2=G (2) | | 11+10=U (4) | |
| | | | | 10+5=O (4) | | |

| | | | | | | |
|---|---|---|---|---|---|---|
| | | | | | 1+0=A (3) | 16+4=T (1) |
| | | 4+1=E (1) | | | 15+8=W (1) | 13+7=T (3) |
| 10+9=S (2) | 14+6=T (2) | 8+6=N (4) | 11+11=V (1) | | 3+2=E (1) | 11+4=O (3) |
| | 10+5=O (4) | 11+4=O (2) | | 6+6=L (1) | 6+2=H (2) | 15+10=Y (3) |
| | 4+5=I (4) | 6+7=M (2) | | 2+1=C (2) | 13+2=O (3) | |
| | 2+1=C (4) | | 1+0=A (2) | | | 10+10=T (3) |
| | | 11+8=S (4) | | | | |

| | | | | | | | |
|---|---|---|---|---|---|---|---|
| 15+4=S (1) | | | | | | | |
| | 3+2=E (1) | | | 10+10=T (1) | 10+4=N (4) | | |
| | 15+7=V (1) | 23+3=Z (2) | 12+2=N (1) | 6+1=G (4) | 4+1=E (1) | 8+1=I (4) | |
| | 7+2=I (2) | 3+2=E (1) | 1+0=A (2) | 16+2=R (3) | 5+0=E (1) | 6+2=H (4) | |
| | 10+4=N (2) | | 4+3=G (2) | 9+5=N (1) | 14+7=U (3) | 15+4=S (4) | |
| 4+1=E (2) | 3+2=E (3) | 2+1=C (3) | 1+0=A (2) | 15+5=T (3) | 14+4=R (4) | 3+2=E (4) | |
| | 2+2=D (3) | | 1+0=A (3) | 12+1=M (2) | | 9+7=P (4) | |

| | | | | | | | |
|---|---|---|---|---|---|---|---|
| | | | 1+1=B (2) | 17+2=S (1) | | | |
| | | 10+5=O (2) | 10+10=T (1) | | 3+2=E (3) | 4+1=E (3) | |
| | | 14+7=U (2) | 4+1=E (1) | 18+4=V (3) | | 7+5=L (3) | |
| | | 6+6=L (2) | 3+2=E (3) | 3+2=E (1) | | | 11+8=S (3) |
| | | 15+4=S (3) | 4+1=E (2) | 14+4=R (1) | 3+1=D (2) | 10+9=S (1) | |
| 11+12=W (4) | | 15+7=V (2) | 16+6=V (4) | 14+4=R (2) | 12+8=T (1) | | |
| | | 1+0=A (4) | 1+0=A (2) | 4+1=E (4) | 10+9=S (4) | | |